THE
COVID
RESPONSE
at Five Years

BROWNSTONE INSTITUTE
Austin, Texas I 2025

BROWNSTONE
INSTITUTE

THE
COVID
RESPONSE
at Five Years

A History of the
End of Civilization

BROWNSTONE
INSTITUTE

FOREWORD

For those who lived through this period, this book is a painful but gripping read. It appeared first at Brownstone.org, chapter by chapter, garnering praise from the world over for its steady tone, granular detail, narrative precision, and moral passion.

The times felt like a blur because normal life was so upended in unthinkable ways. This book operates as a tool of focus as if on a camera lens, turning fuzzy images into clear pictures. Therein lies the pain.

The author is listed as the institutional name because it is true. The results herein are the product of a vast community of researchers, nearly all independent from academia and the science establishment, though many medical practitioners contributed.

Piecing all this together has been herculean and the research behind it all made possible only through tremendous digging and sleuthing. Integrating it all is an achievement.

We wondered about listing names but it is difficult because someone will be left out and it is likely that no single person who contributed is ready to embrace every aspect of the composite text that follows. Everyone has a slightly different spin, different emphasis, and different interpretation of what constitutes the main plots versus extraneous detail.

All that said, this is a credible first draft of a history that legacy institutions want forgotten. We cannot forget, nor allow court historians of the future to pretend as if the last five years were an earnest effort with some mistakes along the way. It was not that at all. It was a studied and concerted effort to end what we once called civilization.

The following thank you will have to suffice: gratitude to Brownstone Institute Fellows, writers, associates, donors, readers, and the countless numbers who have overcome every barrier to share this material with others and feed this fire of truth so that these years will not be erased from the history books.

THE END OF THE PRE-COVID WORLD

"This is the way the world ends," T.S. Eliot wrote in 1925. "Not with a bang but a whimper." Ninety-five years later, the pre-Covid world ended with a nationwide sigh of submission. Democrats remained silent as government mandates transferred trillions of dollars from the working class to tech oligarchs. Republicans dithered as states criminalized church attendance. Libertarians stood by as the nation shuttered the doors of small businesses. College students obediently forfeited their freedoms and moved into their parents' basements, liberals accepted widespread surveillance campaigns, and conservatives greenlit the printing of 300 years' worth of money in sixty days.

With rare exception, March 2020 was a bipartisan, inter-generational capitulation to fear and hysteria. Those who dared to object to the freshly-mandated orthodoxy were subject to widespread contempt, derision, and censorship as the US Security State and a subservient media corps muzzled their protests. The most dominant forces in society used the opportunity to their advantage, pillaging the nation's treasury and overthrowing law and tradition. Their campaign was devoid of the triumph of Yorktown, the bloodshed of Antietam, or the sacrifices of Omaha

1

Beach. Without a single bullet, they overtook the republic, overturning the Bill of Rights in a quiet *coup d'état*.

Perhaps no episode better exemplified this phenomenon than the House of Representatives on March 27, 2020. That day, the House planned to pass the largest spending bill in American history, the CARES Act, without a recorded vote. The $2 trillion price tag was more money than Congress spent on the entire Iraq War, twice as much as the cost of the Vietnam War, and thirteen times more than Congress's annual allocation for Medicaid - all adjusted for inflation. No House Democrats objected, nor did 195 out of 196 House Republicans. For 434 members of the House, there were no concerns of fiscal responsibility or electoral accountability. There wouldn't be a whimper, let alone a bang; there wouldn't even be a recorded vote.

But there was one voice of dissent. When Representative Thomas Massie learned of his colleagues' plan, he drove overnight from Garrison, Kentucky to the Capitol. "I came here to make sure our republic doesn't die by unanimous consent and empty chamber," he announced on the floor.

Democrats, the self-professed guardians of democracy, did not heed his call to fulfill their obligation to represent their constituents. Republicans, supposed defenders of originalism and the rule of law, ignored Massie's invocation of the constitutional requirement for a quorum to be present to conduct business in the House. The supreme law of the land gave way to the hysteria of coronavirus, and the Kentucky Congressman became the target of a bipartisan character assassination.

President Trump called Massie a "third rate Grandstander" and urged Republicans to expel him from the party. John Kerry wrote that Massie had "tested positive for being an asshole" and should be "quarantined to prevent the spread of his massive stupidity." President Trump responded, "Never knew John Kerry had such a good sense of humor! Very impressed!"

Republican Senator Dan Sullivan quipped to Democratic Rep. Sean Patrick Mahoney, "What a dumbass." Mahoney was so proud of the conversation that he took to Twitter. "I can confirm that @RepThomasMassie is indeed a dumbass," he posted.

Two days later, President Trump signed the CARES Act. He bragged that it was the "single-biggest economic relief package in American history." He continued, "It's $2.2 billion, but it actually goes up to 6.2 — potentially — billion dollars — trillion dollars. So you're talking about 6.2 trillion-dollar bill. Nothing like that."

The bipartisan Covid regime stood behind the President smiling. Senator McConnell called it a "proud moment for our country." Rep. Kevin McCarthy and Vice President Pence offered similar praise. Trump thanked Dr. Anthony Fauci, who remarked, "I feel really, really good about what's happening today." Deborah Birx added her support for the bill, as did Secretary of the Treasury Steve Mnuchin. The President then handed Dr. Fauci and others the pens that he used to sign the law. Before leaving, he took time to chastise Rep. Massie again, calling him "totally out of line."

By the end of March 2020, the pre-Covid world was over. Corona was the supreme law of the land.

The Press Conference That Changed the World

On March 16, 2020, Donald Trump, Deborah Birx, and Anthony Fauci held a White House press conference on the coronavirus. After nearly an hour of unremarkable questions and answers, a reporter asked whether the government was suggesting that "bars and restaurants should shut down over the next fifteen days."

President Trump ceded the microphone to Birx. As she stumbled through her answer, Fauci flashed a hand signal to indicate that he wished to step in. He walked to the podium and opened a small document. There was no indication that President Trump knew what was coming next or that he had read the paper.

Is the government calling for a shutdown for 15 days? Fauci took the microphone. "The small print here. It's really small print," he began. President Trump was distracted. He pointed at someone in the audience and appeared unconcerned with Fauci's answer. "America's doctor" continued at the microphone as his boss engaged in a side conversation with someone in the audience.

"In states with evidence of community transmission, bars, restaurants, food courts, gyms and other indoor and outdoor venues where groups of people congregate should be closed." Birx grinned in the background as she listened to the plan to shut down the country. Fauci walked away from the podium, nodded at Birx, and smiled as the press prepared a new question.

The plan that gave them unbridled joy was unprecedented in "public health." Despite firsthand knowledge of smallpox and Yellow Fever, the Framers had not written epidemic contingencies into the Bill of Rights. The nation had not suspended the Constitution for pandemics in 1957 (Hong Kong flu), 1921 (Diphtheria), 1918 (Spanish flu), or 1849 (Cholera). This time, however, it would be different.

The press conference that day was never meant to be a temporary means to *flatten the curve*; it was the beginning, "a first step," toward their vision to "rebuild the infrastructures of human existence," they later admitted. "We worked simultaneously to develop the flattening-the-curve guidance," Birx reflected in her memoir. "Getting buy-in on the simple mitigation measures every American could take was just the first step leading to longer and more aggressive interventions." After demanding that buy-in on March 16, the pre-Covid world was over. *Longer and more aggressive interventions* became reality.

The following day, a branch of the Department of Homeland Security called the Cybersecurity and Infrastructure Security Agency (CISA) released a guide on who was permitted to work and who was subjected to lockdowns. The order divided Americans into two classes: essential and nonessential. Media, Big Tech, and commercial facilities like Costco and Walmart were exempt from the lockdown orders while small businesses, churches, gyms, restaurants, and public schools were shut down. With just one administrative order, America suddenly became an explicitly class-based society in which liberty depended on political favoritism.

On March 21, an image of the Statue of Liberty locked in her apartment appeared on the front page of the *New York Post*. "CITY UNDER LOCKDOWN," the paper announced. States chained playgrounds and criminalized recreation. The schools closed, businesses failed, and hysteria ran rampant.

War Fever

When Massie arrived at the Capitol, a war-like fervor had taken over the country. Publications including *Politico*, ABC, and *The Hill* compared the respiratory virus to the terrorist attacks of September 11, 2001. On March 23, the *New York Times* published "What 9/11 Taught Us About Leadership in a Crisis," offering "lessons for today's leaders" in response to a "similar challenge."

The column did not warn against the dangers of impulsive responses leading to unintended consequences, unaccountable government agencies, unscrupulous ideologues, and untold federal expenditures. There were no analyses of how temporary national fear could lead to trillions of dollars wasted on disastrous initiatives. Instead, the "similar challenge" led to familiar smear campaigns.

Thomas Massie and Barbara Lee have very little in common; Massie, an MIT alumnus, styles himself a "high-tech redneck." His Christmas card featured his family of seven holding guns with the caption "Santa, please bring ammo." Lee, a California Democrat, volunteered for Oakland's Black Panther Party and marched alongside Nancy Pelosi at the "Women's March." Both, however, stood as lone voices of dissent in the two most defining crises of this century. They served as Cassandras, issuing prophetic warnings that drew the ire of disastrous bipartisan consensus.

In September 2001, Lee was the only member of Congress to oppose the authorization to use military force. With the rubble still smoldering at the World Trade Center, she warned Americans that the AUMF provided "a blank check to the president to attack anyone involved in the Sept. 11 events — anywhere, in any country, without regard to our nation's long-term foreign policy, economic and national security interests, and without time limit." A jingoistic press attacked Lee as "un-American," and she received bipartisan condemnation from her peers in Congress.

When Massie took the House floor nineteen years later, American troops were still in Afghanistan, and the "blank check" had been used to support bombings in at least ten other countries. Like Lee, Massie's dissent was prescient. He warned that the Covid payments benefited "banks and corporations" over "working class Americans," that the spending programs were riddled with waste, that the bill transferred dangerous power to an unaccountable Federal Reserve, and that the increased debt would be costly for the American people.

In retrospect, Massie's points were obvious. The Covid response became the most disruptive and destructive public policy in

Western history. The lockdowns destroyed the middle class while the pandemic minted a new billionaire every day. Childhood suicides skyrocketed, and school closures created an educational crisis. People lost jobs, friends, and basic rights for challenging Covid orthodoxy. The Federal Reserve printed three hundred years' worth of spending in two months. The PPP Program cost nearly $300,000 per job "saved," and fraudsters stole $200 billion from Covid relief programs. The federal deficit more than tripled, adding over $3 trillion to the national debt. Studies found the pandemic response will cost Americans $16 trillion over the next decade.

What We Knew Then

Time vindicated Massie, but the pro-lockdown advocates have not demonstrated remorse. To evade responsibility for their catastrophic policies, many cower behind the excuse that *we didn't know then what we know now*. "I think we would've done everything differently," Gavin Newsom reflected in September 2023. "We didn't know what we didn't know." "Let's declare a pandemic amnesty," The *Atlantic* published in October 2022. The precautions may have been "totally misguided," wrote Brown Professor Emily Oster, an advocate for school closures, lockdowns, universal masking, and vaccine mandates. "But the thing is: *We didn't know*."

But the evidence from March 2020 refutes the Rumsfeldian invocation of unknown unknowns.

On February 3, 2020, the Diamond Princess cruise ship was set to return to harbor in Japan. When reports emerged that there had been an outbreak of the novel coronavirus aboard the ship, authorities kept it in the water to quarantine. Suddenly, the ship's 3,700 passengers and crew members became the first contained study of Covid. The *New York Times* described it as a "floating, mini-version of Wuhan." The *Guardian* called it a "coronavirus breeding ground." It remained in quarantine for almost a month, and passengers lived under strict lockdown orders as their community went through the largest outbreak of Covid outside China.

The ship administered over 3,000 PCR tests. By the time the last passengers left the boat on March 1, at least two things were clear: the virus spread rapidly in close quarters, and it posed no significant threat to non-senior citizens.

There were 2,469 passengers on the ship under the age of 70. Zero of them died despite being held on a cruise ship without access to proper medical care. There were over 1,000 people on the ship between 70 and 79. Six died after testing positive for Covid. Out of the 216 people on the ship between 80 and 89, just one died with Covid.

Those points became even more clear in the ensuing weeks.

On March 2, over 800 public health scientists warned against lockdowns, quarantines, and restrictions in an open letter. ABC reported that Covid likely only posed a threat to the elderly. So did *Slate, Haaretz,* and the *Wall Street Journal.* On March 8, Dr. Peter C Gøtzsche wrote that we were "the victims of mass panic," noting that "the average age of those who died after coronavirus infection was 81... [and] they also often had comorbidity."

On March 11, Stanford Professor John Ioannidis published a peer-reviewed paper that warned of "an epidemic of false claims and potentially harmful actions." He predicted the hysteria surrounding the coronavirus would lead to drastically exaggerated case fatality ratios and society-wide collateral damage from unscientific mitigation efforts like lockdowns. "We're falling into a trap of sensationalism," Dr. Ioannidis told interviewers two weeks later. "We have gone into a complete panic state."

On March 13, Michael Burry, the hedge fund manager famously portrayed by Christian Bale in *The Big Short*, tweeted: "With COVID-19, the hysteria appears to me worse than the reality, but after the stampede, it won't matter whether what started it justified it." Ten days later, he wrote: "If COVID-19 testing were universal, the fatality rate would be less than 0.2%," adding that there was no justification "for sweeping government policies, lacking any and all nuance, that destroy the lives, jobs, and businesses of the other 99.8%."

By March 15, there were widespread studies on the mental health ramifications of lockdowns, the health impact of shuttering the economy, and the harms of overreacting to the virus.

Even the Covid regime's wildly inaccurate models, which overestimated the fatality rate of Covid by multitudes, could not justify the response. One of the main bases for lockdown policies was Neil Ferguson's Imperial College London report from March 16. Ferguson's model overestimated the impact of Covid on various age groups by degrees of hundreds but conceded that the young faced no substantial risk from the virus. It predicted a 0.002% fatality rate for ages 0-9 and a 0.006% fatality rate for ages 10-19. For comparison, the fatality rate for the flu "is estimated to be around 0.1%," according to NPR.

On March 20, Yale Professor David Katz wrote in *the New York Times*: "Is Our Fight Against Coronavirus Worse Than the Disease?" He explained:

> "I am deeply concerned that the social, economic and public health consequences of this near total meltdown of normal life — schools and businesses closed, gatherings banned — will be long lasting and calamitous, possibly graver than the direct toll of the virus itself. The stock market will bounce

back in time, but many businesses never will. The unemployment, impoverishment and despair likely to result will be public health scourges of the first order."

He cited data from the Netherlands, the United Kingdom, and South Korea which suggested that 99% of active cases in the general population were "mild" and did not require medical treatment. He referenced the Diamond Princess cruise ship, which housed "a contained, older population," as further proof that the virus appeared harmless to non-senior citizens.

Later that month, Dr. Jay Bhattacharya called for "immediate steps to evaluate the empirical basis of the current lockdowns" in the *Wall Street Journal*. The same week, Ann Coulter published "How do we Flatten the Curve on Panic?" She wrote: "If, as the evidence suggests, the Chinese virus is enormously dangerous to people with certain medical conditions and those over 70 years old, but a much smaller danger to those under 70, then shutting down the entire country indefinitely is probably a bad idea."

Harvard Medical School Professor Dr. Martin Kulldorff wrote in April, "COVID-19 Counter Measures Should be Age Specific." He explained:

"Among COVID-19 exposed individuals, people in their 70s have roughly twice the mortality of those in their 60s, 10 times the mortality of those in their 50s, 40 times that of those in their 40s, 100 times that of those in their 30s, 300 times that of those in their 20s, and a mortality that is more than 3000 times higher than for children. Since COVID-19 operates in a highly age specific manner, mandated counter measures must also be age specific. If not, lives will be unnecessarily lost."

On April 7, Burry called on states to lift their lockdown orders, which he decried as "ruining innumerable lives in a criminally unjust manner." On April 9, Dr. Joseph Ladapo, who later became the Surgeon General of Florida, wrote in the *Wall Street Journal*: "Lockdowns Won't Stop the Spread." Ten days later, Georgia Governor Brian Kemp reopened his state. "Our next measured step is driven by data and guided by state public health officials," Kemp explained. Shortly thereafter, Governor Ron DeSantis lifted Covid restrictions in Florida.

Brian Kemp, Thomas Massie, and Ron DeSantis didn't flip a coin on the Covid issue. They knew they'd be accused of endangering fellow citizens, killing grandmas, and overrunning the healthcare system. If they nodded along to the consensus like their peers, then they could have increased their power and perhaps won an Emmy like Andrew Cuomo. Joining the herd was socially and politically fashionable, but their rationality stood athwart the prevailing madness.

Wisdom was in short supply in American government and media. Anthony Fauci and President Trump attacked Kemp for reopening Georgia. The *New York Times* stoked racial animus to criticize opponents of the Covid regime, telling its readers that "black residents" would have to "bear the brunt" of Kemp's decision to "reopen many businesses over objections from President Trump and others." The *New York Daily News* referred to "Florida Morons" daring to go to the beach that summer, and the *Washington Post*, *Newsweek*, and MSNBC chastised "DeathSantis." While the slanders and hysteria were temporary, a radical and insidious movement sought to permanently transform the country.

The Quiet Coup

Amid the name-calling and memorable headlines of school closures, arrests for paddle boarding, and urban anarchy, the nation underwent a *coup d'état* in 2020. The First Amendment and freedom of speech were replaced by a censorship operation designed to silence citizens. The Fourth Amendment was supplanted by a system of mass surveillance. Jury trials and the Seventh Amendment disappeared in favor of government-provided legal immunity for the nation's most powerful political force. Americans found they suddenly lived under a police state without the freedom to travel. Due process disappeared as the government issued edicts to determine who could and could not work. Equal application of the law was a relic of the past as a self-appointed caste of Brahmins exempted themselves and their political allies from the authoritarian orders that applied to the masses.

The groups that implemented this system also benefited from it. State and federal government agencies gained tremendous power. Unshackled from the restraints of the Bill of Rights, they used the pretext of "public health" to reshape society and abolish personal liberties. Social media giants assisted these efforts, using their power to silence critics of the new Leviathan. Big Pharma enjoyed record profits and government-provided legal immunity. In just one year, the Covid response transferred over $3.7 trillion from the working class to billionaires. To replace our liberties, Big Government, Big Tech, and Big Pharma offer a new ruling order of suppression of dissent, surveillance of the masses, and indemnity of the powerful.

The hegemonic triumvirate framed their agenda with favorable marketing strategies. Eviscerating the First Amendment became *monitoring misinformation*. Warrantless surveillance fell under the public health umbrella of *contact tracing*. The fusion of corporate and state power advertised itself as *public-private partnerships*. House arrest received a social media rebranding of #stayathomesavelives. Within months, business owners replaced their "We stand with first responders" signs with "Going out of business" announcements.

Once the rule of law had been overturned, the culture was soon to follow.

Ten weeks after the press conference that changed the world, a Minnesota police officer put his knee on the neck of a Covid-infected, fentanyl-laced career criminal. This led to cardiopulmonary arrest, the death of the man, and a cultural revolution. The BLM and Antifa violent protests in reaction to the death of George Floyd sparked 120 days of rioting and looting in the summer of 2020. Over 35 people died, 1,500 police officers were injured, and rioters caused $2 billion in property damage. CNN covered the resulting arson in Wisconsin with the chyron "FIERY BUT MOSTLY PEACEFUL PROTESTS."

With the notable exception of Senator Tom Cotton, politicians were largely complicit in the mass looting and violence. President Trump was absent; while the cities burned on the weekend of May 30, the Commander-in-Chief was uncharacteristically silent. His only communication was that the Secret Service had kept him and his family safe.

Others seemed to encourage the destruction. Kamala Harris raised money to pay bail for looters and rioters arrested in Minneapolis. Tim Walz's wife, then Minnesota's First Lady, told the press that she "kept the windows open as long as [she] could" in order to smell "the burning" from the riots. Nikki Haley tweeted, "the death of George Floyd was personal and painful for many. In order to heal, it needs to be personal and painful for everyone."

And painful it was. Just hours before Haley's demand for

communal suffering, rioters set fire to Minneapolis's Third Precinct police building. Thousands celebrated around the building as it burned. They looted the evidence rooms as the police inside fled under the mayor's orders. Two days later, the mobs in St. Louis killed 77-year-old former policeman David Dorn. His death was broadcast on Facebook Live.

Every major institution cowered to the demands of the rising Jacobins. Once proud institutions released statements of self-flagellation, statues of American heroes came toppling down, and crime skyrocketed. In Minnesota alone, aggravated assault increased 25%, robberies increased 26%, arson increased 54%, and murder increased 58%. Vandals toppled Minneapolis's statue of George Washington and covered it in paint. Minnesota State University removed its statue of Abraham Lincoln from its campus display after 100 years after students complained that it perpetuated *systemic racism.*

None of this concerned the truth behind Floyd's death. Typically, deaths in individuals with fentanyl concentrations over 3 ng/ml are considered overdoses. Floyd's toxicology report revealed 11 ng/ml of fentanyl, 5.6 ng/ml of norfentanyl, and 19 ng/ml of methamphetamine. Floyd's autopsy concluded that there were "no life-threatening injuries identified," and the county medical examiner told the local prosecutor that there "were no medical indications of asphyxia or strangulation." He asked, "What happens when the actual evidence doesn't match up with the public narrative that everyone's already decided on?"

Evidently, the answer was a nationwide cultural upheaval. The wreckage spread through the country and beyond June 2020. The racial reckoning left no American institution untouched. "New homicide records were set in 2021 in Philadelphia, Columbus, Indianapolis, Rochester, Louisville, Toledo, Baton Rouge, St.

Paul, Portland, and elsewhere," Heather MacDonald writes in *When Race Trumps Merit*. "The violence continued into 2022. January 2022 was Baltimore's deadliest month in nearly 50 years." New York City removed statues of Thomas Jefferson and Teddy Roosevelt; California vagrants toppled tributes to Ulysses S. Grant, Francis Scott Key, and Francis Drake; San Francisco vandals dragged statues and prepared to toss them into a fountain until they learned the fountain was a memorial to AIDS victims. Oregon criminals desecrated statues of T.R., Abraham Lincoln, and George Washington.

At Rockefeller University, they removed the portraits of scientists who won the Nobel Prize because they were white men. The University of Pennsylvania took down a portrait of William Shakespeare because it failed to "affirm their commitment to a more inclusive mission for the English Department." The soon-to-be 46th President and his allies announced that there would be racial prerequisites for the selection of its highest-ranking officials – including the Vice President, a Supreme Court Justice, and the Senator from California. The private sector was even worse: in the year after the George Floyd riots, just 6% of new S&P jobs went to white applicants, a result that required mass discrimination.

By Independence Day 2020, the coup d'état had succeeded. The rule of law had been overturned. Former bedrock principles of the Republic – freedom of speech, freedom to travel, freedom from surveillance – were sacrificed upon the altar of public health. A culture that had once championed meritocracy became obsessed with berating the identity of the majority of its population. Hypocrisy in the ruling class grew to the point that there was no longer equal application of the law. The most powerful groups augmented their wealth while the working class suffered under despotism.

This series is meant to outline the freedoms that we sacrificed, and, just as importantly, the people and institutions that benefited from the erosion of our liberties. There are no allegations of the pandemic's causes. Those speculations, intriguing as they may be, are unnecessary to demonstrate the coordinated upheaval that took place. The bedrocks of liberty enshrined in the Bill of Rights disappeared while the nation panicked. The most powerful people profited while the weakest suffered. Under the pretense of "public health," the Republic was overturned.

THE FIRST AMENDMENT VS.
THE U.S. SECURITY STATE

The Covid regime's assault on the First Amendment reads like a plotline out of a Robert Ludlum novel. A virus emerged from the shores of a foreign adversary and spawned a domestic crisis. Government bureaucrats seized the opportunity to expand their power. They launched interagency campaigns to coerce private actors to carry out their orders. They nationalized the country's private information centers, dictating what their citizens could read or write about the emergency that triggered their newfound authority.

Later, their true interests became clear: the chief censors were implicated in the creation of the virus, and they orchestrated a cover-up to hide their culpability. Working with the Intelligence Community, they bribed scientists to alter their published opinions. They targeted journalists for deviating from their party line. Their colleagues bought "burner phones" to delete any record of communication. They held secret meetings at the CIA and the State Department. They avoided government emails to keep their leader's "fingerprints" off the incriminating evidence. Their cabal created an international shadow government, dictating policy designed to evade accountability for their past misdeeds.

If that sounds like a conspiracy, it's because it was. The public health apparatus, the White House, and the Intelligence Community spearheaded a coordinated attack on free expression in the United States. They launched coercive campaigns to nationalize our news sources, and they stripped Americans of their First Amendment rights to augment their power. This informational stranglehold required technological power that sparked, as Justice Neil Gorsuch later wrote, possibly "the greatest intrusions on civil liberties in the peacetime history of this country."

. . .

The advent of the internet promised a liberation. The free flow of information appeared inevitable. Connectivity seemed emancipatory. Autocracies would be unable to control the emerging swell of information. Social media would create a digital community where users could interact without government interference.

"There's no question China has been trying to crack down on the internet," President Clinton remarked in 2000. "Good luck. That's sort of like trying to nail Jell-O to the wall."

In the second half of the 20th century, the First Amendment had ascended to a status of secular scripture in the United States. Hollywood deified journalists, and the ACLU defended free speech for all citizens, especially those with the least popular views. In 1989, the Supreme Court wrote: "If there is a bedrock principle underlying the First Amendment, it is that the government may not prohibit the expression of an idea simply because society finds the idea itself offensive or disagreeable."

The internet became the frontier of free expression in the ensuing decades. Americans thought the First Amendment separated them from autocracies' digital book burning. In China, the state curated citizens' newsfeeds to ensure compliance with government orthodoxy. The "Great Firewall" denied users access to websites outside the CCP's control. Westerners joined President Clinton's optimism that authoritarianism would cave to the force of the internet. The 2012 Democratic National Platform declared, "President Obama is strongly committed to protecting an open Internet that fosters investment, innovation, creativity, consumer choice, and free speech, unfettered by censorship or undue violations of privacy."

That optimism soon disappeared; the U.S. Security State and D.C. bureaucrats weaponized technological advances against the First Amendment after transgressive cyber actors like Edward Snowden and Julian Assange exposed the vastness of their crimes. Now, online censorship is an unavoidable reality rather than an abstract analogy. The internet did not secure free speech rights; it augmented governments' ability to crack down on dissidents. Technology did not liberate the oppressed; it created a global panopticon that captured citizens' information and implemented unprecedented surveillance. Connectivity did not unleash a flourishment of freedom; it centralized power more than ever before. The powers of the web did not lead to an Enlightenment-inspired Westernization of the Orient; the United States adopted the most totalitarian pillars of the Chinese regime.

In just eight years, the Democratic Party's official platform shifted from vowing to protect an internet "unfettered by censorship" to announcing that it would take action to combat "disinformation" and technology that helped "spread hate," however party officials defined those terms.

In the response to Covid, the federal government overturned the First Amendment's "bedrock principle." The United States, in tandem with its partners in Silicon Valley, censored dissent, targeted inconvenient journalists, and worked toward a Chinese system of state-curated newsfeeds. Doctors faced gag orders and career-threatening punishment for treating their patients. The Covid regime reframed discourse as a threat, rather than a prerequisite, to democracy. The promise of the internet had died, and the United States had abandoned its founding principles.

The institutions and individuals who championed the crackdown on free speech acted in self-interest. They hijacked the scientific method and subordinated the First Amendment to the interests of federal bureaucrats and campaign donors. In brazen disregard for the concept of self-government, they funneled taxpayer funds to bribe parties into toeing the line of government-sponsored propaganda. The origin of this process can be traced to an email from January 2020.

The Proximal Origin of Pandemic Censorship - 01/27/2020 – 6:24 pm

January 27, 2020 was a Monday. Most news coverage focused on the death of Kobe Bryant the previous day in a helicopter accident. John Bolton appeared on morning shows to speak against President Trump as the Senate considered his first impeachment trial. The CDC confirmed the fifth case of Covid-19 in the United States, and the *New York Times* featured two front-page stories on the rise of the Chinese coronavirus.

Below the fold, a photograph showed men in hazmat suits exiting a medical facility. "Hospitals in Wuhan, China, the epicenter of the coronavirus outbreak, remain intensely crowded," the caption read. Viral videos circulated the internet showing men and women collapsing in the streets. Though later proven false, they were the center of an ominous news cycle. The victims suddenly fell to the ground as masked paramedics rushed to their aid. "It is an image that captures the chilling reality of the coronavirus outbreak in the Chinese city of Wuhan," the *Guardian* reported. "A grey-haired man wearing a face mask lies dead on the pavement, a plastic shopping bag in one hand, as police and medical staff in full protective suits and masks prepare to take him away."

More responsible figures explained that the virus appeared to only affect the elderly and those with severe comorbidities, but the headlines induced panic-stricken Americans to stock up on household supplies and canned goods.

Anthony Fauci's panic that day was more personal. At 6:24 pm, he received an email warning that he could be implicated in the origin of the virus sweeping through China. His assistant at the NIAID, Greg Folkers, relayed concerns that the agency had funded research on coronaviruses at the Wuhan Institute of Virology through grants it made to EcoHealth Alliance, an American nonprofit group led by Peter Daszak. That research, Folkers warned, could be the source of Covid. The email included a study from virologist Ralph Baric warning that gain-of-function research on coronaviruses could create "SARS 2.0."

Folkers suggested that the United States government, through Anthony Fauci's grants, had funded what came to be known as the "lab-leak" hypothesis. If true, it threatened political ruin and legal exposure for Fauci. Folkers wrote: "NIAID has funded Peter [Daszak]'s group for coronavirus work in China for the past 5 years...Collaborators include Wuhan Institute of Virology."

After four decades in government, Fauci had reached the apex of his power. He was the highest paid government official in the United States, drawing a salary 20% higher than the President's, and he controlled billions of dollars in federal grants. He was a newly minted media celebrity and the face of American public health. That week, he began advertising to journalists that a new vaccine for the coronavirus was in development. Now, Folkers warned that he may be responsible for funding the creation of the virus that would define his career.

Fauci risked more than mere embarrassment. Six years earlier, President Obama had suspended all funding for "gain-of-function research" (a process whereby scientists genetically alter viruses) after critics warned that the engineered viruses could escape laboratories. The Obama White House issued a moratorium in response to concerns regarding "biosafety incidents at federal research facilities." But Fauci's public health bureaucracy had not heeded President Obama's ban; instead, they helped groups continue their forbidden research.

Fauci had been a longtime advocate for gain-of-function research. In 2012, he published an eerily prescient article in its defense. He wrote that even if a "scientist becomes infected with the virus, which leads to an outbreak and ultimately triggers a pandemic," the "benefits of such experiments and the resulting knowledge [would still] outweigh the risks."

Fauci's chief ally at the *New York Times*, Donald McNeil (one of the most ardent advocates for extreme lockdowns beginning in February 2020), later defended U.S. funding of gain-of-function research at the Wuhan Institute of Virology *even if* it sparked the pandemic. "Let me say this bluntly," he wrote in April 2023. "Supporting the bat research done by EcoHealth Alliance and the Wuhan Institute of Virology was the right thing to do."

As head of the NIAID, Fauci issued grants to coronavirus researchers like EcoHealth Alliance despite the Obama prohibition. In May 2016, two NIH staff members alerted Peter Daszak that his group's experiments "appear to involve research covered under the pause," referring to President Obama's gain-of-function moratorium. Instead of enforcing the government order, the NIH helped Daszak evade the restrictions of the ban, rewriting EcoHealth Alliance's grant requests and safety documentation. EcoHealth continued its gain-of-function research on coronaviruses and entered ongoing partnerships with the Wuhan Institute of Virology. Upon receiving a grant that year, Daszak emailed NIH officials: "This is terrific! We are very happy to hear that our Gain of Function research funding pause has been lifted."

In a February 2020 *New York Times* article, Daszak explained how his group began research in 2018 on "an unknown, novel pathogen that hadn't yet entered the human population." He wrote that this disease "would probably be confused with other diseases early in the outbreak and would spread quickly and silently; exploiting networks of human travel and trade, it would reach multiple countries and thwart containment." He continued, "[it] would have a mortality rate higher than a seasonal flu but would spread as easily as the flu." Government documents later revealed that Daszak requested $14 million from the Pentagon to make viruses with unique features of SARS-CoV-2 in Wuhan in 2018.

By January 27, 2020, that *novel pathogen* appeared to have arrived. At 6:24 pm, Folkers warned that Fauci could be implicated in the most widespread public health scandal in world history. The email detailed how Fauci provided Daszak and EcoHealth Alliance with millions of taxpayer dollars, and that their "collaborators include Wuhan Institute of Virology." A government audit later concluded: "Despite identifying potential risks associated with research being performed under the EcoHealth awards... NIH did not effectively monitor or take timely action to address EcoHealth's compliance with some requirements."

The panic circled the global public health apparatus that day. Fauci's British counterpart – Wellcome Trust Director Jeremy

Farrar – started his own cover-up campaign. Farrar ordered a "burner phone" on January 27 when he realized that the Western health community may be implicated in the origins of the virus. "I now had a burner phone, which I would use only for this purpose and then get rid of," he wrote in his memoir. He told his wife, "We should use different phones; avoid putting things in emails; and ditch our normal email addresses and phone contacts."

By early that evening, Fauci and Farrar both knew they could be implicated in the emergence of the virus. They shared a defensive reaction. They issued no *mea culpa*, no explanation to the public on the dangers of gain-of-function research, no call to investigate the Wuhan Institute of Virology. Instead, they launched a coordinated censorship campaign to ostracize anyone questioning the origins of the virus or lending credence to the lab-leak hypothesis. The proximal origin of Covid censorship was a primal instinct of self-preservation. Their careers depended on its success.

Fauci and Farrar recruited virologists Kristian Andersen and Eddie Holmes to join their efforts. On January 29, Andersen warned Farrar that the coronavirus may have emerged from gain-of-function research. Andersen focused on a paper that he described as a "how-to manual for building the Wuhan coronavirus in a laboratory." It outlined how scientists could engineer a bat coronavirus to infect humans.

"Andersen found a scientific paper where exactly this technique had been used to modify the spike protein of the original SARS-CoV-1 virus, the one that had caused the SARS outbreak of 2002/3," Farrar wrote in his memoir. "The pair knew of a laboratory where researchers had been experimenting on coronaviruses for years: the Wuhan Institute of Virology, in the city at the heart of the outbreak."

Farrar then emailed Fauci requesting to speak to him privately over the phone. Andersen joined their call, and they organized a series of secret teleconferences that week. After Andersen raised his concerns surrounding the Wuhan Institute of Virology, Dr. Fauci prompted "Proximal Origin," an initiative to disprove the lab-leak theory before it reached the public. They had inverted the scientific method; their predetermined conclusion would guide their research. Virologists repeatedly warned Fauci that the virus was "inconsistent with expectations from evolutionary theory," but their job evolved into a mission to reverse-engineer a zoonotic thesis.

Dr. Robert Redfield, who served as head of the Centers for Disease Control and Prevention from 2018 to 2021, later testified that he warned Fauci and colleagues as early as January 2020 that the virus appeared to have emerged from a laboratory rather than jumping from animals to humans. He argued that the virus's "furin-cleavage" site – a spot in which the virus's proteins can make it infect human cells more easily – suggested human manipulation. For voicing these concerns, Dr. Fauci excluded Redfield from all discussions concerning the origin of the virus.

Redfield was not alone in his concerns. In late January, Kristian Andersen texted colleague Eddie Holmes, "Eddie, can we talk? I need to be pulled off a ledge here," after he discovered the furin-cleavage site and worried that it was evidence of gain-of-function research.

As Fauci received ongoing warnings that the virus appeared to be engineered, the pressure mounted. Investigators would not have to look far to find the publicly available information: Fauci's institute had funded gain-of-function research at a laboratory in the epicenter of the outbreak of a virus with unnatural characteristics. The secret teleconferences lasted late into the night. "It's hard to come off nocturnal calls about the possibility of a lab leak and go back to bed," Farrar wrote about the clandestine communications from that period. "Just a few of us – Eddie [Holmes], Kristian [Andersen], Tony [Fauci] and I – were now privy to sensitive information that, if proved to be true, might set off a whole series of events that would be far bigger than any of us. It felt as if a storm was gathering."

The storm continued along its path the following day. On February 1, *Science Magazine* published an article questioning the origins of the virus. The piece cited Andersen and colleagues who expressed concerns about the Wuhan Institute of Virology. Fauci read the article and forwarded it to Andersen, saying it was "of interest to the current discussion."

Within an hour, Farrar and Fauci organized another emergency teleconference. Andersen presented evidence suggesting that the virus emerged from a lab leak. He referenced five studies on gain-of-function research and coronaviruses, all co-authored by Ralph Baric. Baric, however, was excluded from the discussions because they thought he was "too close" to the Wuhan Institute of Virology.

After the call, Fauci requested more information on which projects his agency had funded in Wuhan. Virologists said that they were up to 80 percent certain that the coronavirus came from a lab. Andersen said he agreed with 60 to 70 percent confidence. "I think the main thing still in my mind is that the lab escape version of this is so friggin' likely to have happened because they were already doing this type of work and the molecular data is fully consistent with that scenario," he wrote to colleagues in February.

But there were political concerns that were incompatible with their scientific analysis. "Given the shit show that would happen if anyone serious accused the Chinese of even accidental release, my feeling is we should say that given there is no evidence of a specifically engineered virus, we cannot possibly distinguish between natural evolution and escape so we are content with ascribing it to [a] natural process," Andersen's colleague, Dr. Andrew Rambaut, wrote in their Slack group in February 2020. Fauci worked to cover his tracks, searching through projects he had funded that could be responsible.

Andersen and a team of virologists worked with Fauci to draft a paper in response to the *Science Magazine* article. Emails later exposed the deliberate cover-up behind the paper. One Fauci advisor revealed that they worked to evade the Freedom of Information Act by avoiding government email accounts. "Tony doesn't want his fingerprints on origin stories...Don't worry...I will delete anything I don't want to see in the *New York Times*."

Andersen and his team thanked Farrar and Fauci for their "advice and leadership," and they pushed forward with their cover-up. They bypassed traditional review periods to publish their article one month later in *Nature Journal*. Their finished product – "The Proximal Origin of SARS-CoV-2" – became the basis for the regime's talking points and censorship efforts. Its thesis was irreconcilable with the authors' conclusions from four weeks earlier.

"We do not believe that any type of laboratory-based scenario is plausible," the article concluded. While Andersen had presented Fauci with extensive evidence that the virus was "inconsistent with expectations from evolutionary theory," his new paper made no mention of his earlier concerns. Later reports revealed that the article underwent significant changes during the drafting period. In February, the authors referenced concerns about the Wuhan Institute of Virology and calls with Ralph Baric and Peter Daszak. Between January 31 and February 28, Andersen and his colleagues made over 50 direct statements that expressed their belief that a lab leak was the likely origin of the virus. "The main issue is that accidental escape [from a lab] is in fact highly likely – it's not some fringe theory," Andersen told colleagues on February 2. Two days later, however, Andersen told the group that Fauci had called another meeting and that "a statement about this not being engineering should be coming out" from their work product.

After three weeks of compiling arguments to assure the public that the virus had natural origins, Andersen emailed his colleagues, "None of this helps refute a lab origin." The final publication, however, removed all references to sources that lent support to the lab-leak hypothesis. Even four weeks *after* the publication of the "Proximal Origin" paper, Andersen remarked privately over text that the scientists "can't fully rule out engineering (for basic research)" as the cause of the virus. Behind closed doors, the scientists repeatedly contradicted their professed belief that they did "not believe that any type of laboratory-based scenario is plausible."

The CIA, Mass Media, and Academia Back the Coverup

In just one month, the authors reversed their conclusions and produced a paper that shielded the public health apparatus from blame for the outbreak of the disease. On February 6, Andersen changed the name of the Slack channel from "Project-Wuhan Engineering" to "Project-Wuhan Pangolin" as the World Health Organization declared that the virus emerged from bats or pangolins (mammals resembling anteaters). Andersen admitted to his colleagues, "For all I know, people could have infected the pangolin, not the other way," but that they had a political narrative to protect.

At the time, Fauci acknowledged the gain-of-function research taking place in China. In February 2020, he wrote to NIH officials, "Scientists in Wuhan University are known to have been working on gain of function experiments to determine the molecular mechanisms associated with bat viruses adapting to human infection, and the outbreak originated in Wuhan." Within weeks, however, scientists abandoned their research into the common-sense link between the virus and gain-of-function research.

What could have prompted their change of heart? A whistle-blower later revealed that the CIA offered payments to scientists to bury findings supporting the lab-leak hypothesis. The House Oversight Committee explained: "According to the whistleblower, at the end of its review, six of the seven members of the Team believed the intelligence and science were sufficient to make a low confidence assessment that COVID-19 originated from a laboratory in Wuhan, China." Then, however, the whistleblower reported that the "six members were given a significant monetary incentive to change their position."

Subsequent reports suggest that the Intelligence Community had strong interests in deploying assets to protect the Wuhan Institute of Virology. Seymour Hersh revealed that the CIA had a spy at the Wuhan Institute of Virology who warned in late 2019 that "China was doing both offensive and defensive work" with pathogens, and that there had been a laboratory accident that resulted in the infection of a researcher.

The Intelligence Community then became central to the cover-up. A whistleblower revealed that Fauci entered CIA head-quarters "without a record of entry" to "influence its Covid-19 origins investigation" early in the pandemic. America's leading public health official was holding clandestine meetings at Langley to steer its investigations away from implicating him in the origin of the virus, and they used taxpayer funding to bribe scientists into subservience. He later held similar meetings with the State Department and the White House.

"Fauci came to our building, to promote the natural origin of the virus," the CIA whistleblower said. "He knew what was going on...He was covering his ass and he was trying to do it with the Intel community...He came multiple times and he was treated like a rock star by the Weapons and Counter Proliferation Mission Center."

It had all the hallmarks of a cover-up. They bought "burner phones" and made sure to limit what they put in writing. They worked to publicize a theory that contradicted everything they discussed behind closed doors. They bribed scientists to purchase their subservience. The Intelligence Community used taxpayer funds to deceive the American public. Then, the cabal worked to silence all dissent on the issue.

Beginning in April, Dr. Fauci told reporters that Covid was "totally consistent with a jump of a species from an animal to a human." He emailed journalists the "Proximal Origin" paper as the basis for his statement. The CIA-funded article became a cudgel to attack anyone who questioned Fauci's authority.

In February 2020, Senator Tom Cotton noticed that the pandemic originated in the same city where a virology lab conducted experiments on coronaviruses. The official narrative didn't add up, he explained on Fox News. There was no evidence linking the original Covid patients to local "wet markets," and Beijing was unwilling to cooperate with investigators. "We don't know where it originated, and we have to get to the bottom of that," Cotton said. "We also know that just a few miles away from that food market is China's only biosafety level 4 super laboratory that researches human infectious diseases."

The *Washington Post* told readers that Cotton had espoused a "fringe" conspiracy theory and quoted a Rutgers Professor Richard Ebright, who assured the audience that there was "absolutely nothing in the genome sequence of this virus that indicates the virus was engineered." A group of Democratic Congressmen accused him of perpetuating "racist stereotypes."

But Cotton's statement was entirely consistent with Andersen's message to Fauci that the "lab escape" was "so friggin' likely to have happened because they were already doing this type of work." Andersen even sent a Slack message to the Proximal Origin authors on February 17 saying that Cotton's theory wasn't "totally wrong." Jeremy Farrar later admitted: "my starting bias was that it was odd for a spillover event, from animals to humans, to take off in people so immediately and spectacularly - in a city with a biolab...This novel virus, spreading like wildfire, seemed almost designed to infect human cells." CDC Director Robert Redfield had the same instinct. "When Redfield saw the breakdown of early cases, some of which were family clusters, the market explanation made less sense. Had multiple family members gotten sick via contact with the same animal?" *Vanity Fair* reported. "Redfield immediately thought of the Wuhan Institute of Virology."

Yet, that discourse was suddenly impermissible in public in the United States under Fauci's leadership. Internal Facebook messages revealed that the federal government worked with social media companies to silence any concerns, reports, or questions like those that Senator Cotton raised. They sought to end the discussion before it led to investigations. Meta, the corporate parent to Instagram and Facebook, banned all posts suggesting that the virus came from a lab. China joined the crackdown on speech. Beijing jailed journalists for challenging the government's narrative of the emergence of the virus. In Wuhan and Washington, discussing the origin of the virus was off-limits.

On April 16, 2020, NIH Director Francis Collins emailed Fauci a report by Fox News host Bret Baier stating that multiple sources believed Covid-19 emerged from the Wuhan Lab. "Wondering if there is something NIH can do to help put down this very destructive conspiracy, with what seems to be growing momentum," wrote Collins. "I hoped the *Nature Medicine* article on the genomic sequence of SARS-CoV-2 would settle this…" Collins didn't specify that the "conspiracy" was only "very destructive" for those that it implicated.

The *Wall Street Journal* later reported that Defense Department experts conducted a genomic analysis in Spring 2020 that found evidence of human manipulation of the virus, which was conducted with the specific techniques utilized at the Wuhan Institute of Virology. These experts, however, were directed by their bosses at the Pentagon to cease sharing their findings. In May 2020, the Defense Department experts wrote an unclassified paper detailing their findings, but they were promptly banned from participating in any briefings with the White House.

Despite clear intelligence pointing to the lab leak (all of which was known by Andersen, Farrar, and Fauci), the Government ramped up its censorship efforts, using the "Proximal Origin" paper from *Nature Medicine* to quash dissent. At the Government's behest, billions of users of Facebook, Instagram, and Twitter were prohibited from mentioning a lab leak online. The information centers banned news accounts, political activists, and virologists from challenging their preferred narrative.

The U.S. House Select Subcommittee on the Coronavirus Pandemic summarized the censorship of the origins of the virus as "the anatomy of a cover-up."

"On January 31, 2020, Dr. Fauci prompted Proximal Origin, which's goal was to 'disprove' the lab leak theory to avoid blaming China for the COVID-19 pandemic. Proximal

Origin employed fatally flawed science to achieve its goal. And, finally, Dr. Collins and Dr. Fauci used Proximal Origin to attempt to kill the lab leak theory. This is the anatomy of a cover-up."

The email from 6:24 pm on January 27 sparked a chain of events that led to the censorship of hundreds of millions of Americans. Citizens lost their right to question, investigate, or discuss the cause of the most disruptive political event in world history. There was no public health basis for the assault on free inquiry; Fauci and his cohorts launched their attack on the lab-leak hypothesis to protect themselves. They used their credentials to bully the press corps and the scientific community into submission. Through their allies in the media, they derided dissent as "fringe theories" that threatened a "dangerous" "infodemic" of "debunked claims."

On MSNBC, Joy Reid called the lab-leak theory "debunked bunkum." CNN reporters referred to it as "widely debunked." Glenn Kessler, a "fact checker" at the *Washington Post*, claimed it was "virtually impossible for this virus to escape from the lab... We deal in facts."

The "Proximal Origin" paper deliberately skewed its findings to support Dr. Fauci's pronouncement that the virus originated in bats. Fauci hid his involvement in the drafting of the paper and the financial offers that the authors received from the CIA. He later testified that he "did not recall" specifics on Covid origins over 100 times in one day of closed-door testimony. In July 2023, the House Oversight Committee held a hearing on "Investigating the Proximal Origin of a Cover Up" to examine the "suppression of scientific discourse" surrounding the March 2020 paper. The Committee found that the co-authors of the paper – including

Andersen and Holmes – abandoned scientific integrity "in favor of political expediency." Rep. Ronny Jackson confronted Andersen about his capitulation to Fauci's interests.

> "You completely changed your hypothesis. You collaborated with your coauthors and you wrote the Proximal Origins paper all in that period of time....I just want you to know that sounds completely ridiculous to the American people. And it's completely in step with what a lot of people think is going on here, is that Dr. Anthony Fauci and Francis Collins realized that they had been implicated in the production or in the creation of this virus. And they were doing everything they could, including getting both of you to come on board as tools or vehicles to undermine that theory."

The censors' driving purpose was to protect their self-interest. They usurped citizens' rights to participate in their government, and their benevolent excuses of "public health" were facades for their tyrannical aspirations. The proximal origin of pandemic censorship revealed the central tenets of the censorship regime: suppression, collusion, and deception designed to evade accountability and augment power. Perhaps more alarmingly, it laid the groundwork for the interagency censorship from the American Intelligence Community.

"The Most Massive Attack Against Free Speech in United States' History"

The scope of the ensuing attack on the First Amendment was unprecedented. President Woodrow Wilson jailed socialist presidential candidate Eugene Debs and had his Postmaster General halt the mailing of dissident political magazines. President John

Adams led the crusade of the Sedition Act against his political opponents. No previous challenge to free expression, however, had the technological reach or the sophistication of the Security State in the Covid response.

In 2023, a group of doctors, journalists, and states sued the Biden administration for alleged violations of their First Amendment rights in *Missouri v. Biden*, later named *Murthy v. Missouri* on appeal. The plaintiffs in the case included doctors Aaron Kheriaty, Martin Kulldorff, Jay Bhattacharya, state attorneys general from Missouri and Louisiana, and independent news outlets. Dr. Bhattacharya, a Stanford professor, co-author of the Great Barrington Declaration (which criticized the United States' lockdown policies), swore under oath that he and his colleagues faced a "relentless covert campaign of social-media censorship of our dissenting view from the government's preferred message" during the Covid response.

Defendants included the Biden White House, the FBI, the CIA, and the Department of Homeland Security. On July 4, 2023, the District Court granted a preliminary injunction in the case that barred defendants from colluding with social media companies to abridge constitutionally protected speech.

"The present case arguably involves the most massive attack against free speech in United States' history," wrote U.S. District Judge Terry Doughty. He continued, "The evidence produced thus far depicts an almost dystopian scenario...The United States Government seems to have assumed a role similar to an Orwellian 'Ministry of Truth.'"

The Government appealed, but the Fifth Circuit largely affirmed Judge Doughty's decision. "The Supreme Court has rarely been faced with a coordinated campaign of this magnitude orchestrated by federal officials that jeopardized a fundamental aspect of American life," the Circuit Court held. The Government, the Court found, "engaged in a years-long pressure campaign designed to ensure that the censorship [on social media] aligned with the government's preferred viewpoint."

The campaign was not limited to rogue government actors; it was a coordinated interagency conspiracy that could be traced to the U.S. Security State and the top of the Biden administration.

"The highest (and I mean the highest) levels of the White House"

The Biden White House, led by Director of Digital Strategy Rob Flaherty, demanded Big Tech suppress political opponents' speech and used the threat of government retaliation to strip citizens of their First Amendment rights.

"Are you guys fucking serious?" Flaherty asked Facebook after the company failed to censor critics of the Covid vaccine. "I want an answer on what happened here and I want it today." At other times, Flaherty was more direct. "Please remove this account immediately," he told Twitter about a Biden family parody account. The company compiled within an hour.

Flaherty made it clear that he was concerned with political power, not veracity or *disinformation*. He demanded Facebook stifle *malinformation*, "often-true content" that could be considered "sensational." He asked company executives if they could interfere with private messages containing "misinformation" on WhatsApp.

Flaherty later demanded to know how Facebook would address "things that are dubious, but not provably false." In February 2021, he accused the company of fomenting "political violence" by allowing "vaccine skeptical" content on its platform.

His desire to control Americans' access to information meant eliminating critical media sources. He demanded Facebook reduce the spread of Tucker Carlson's report on the Johnson & Johnson's vaccine's link to blood clots. "There's 40,000 shares on the video. Who is seeing it now? How many?" Flaherty's attack on the First Amendment was not directed at the speaker – the objective was to protect political power by denying citizens the right to access information.

"I'm curious – NY Post churning out articles every day about people dying," he wrote to Facebook. "Does that article get a reduction, labels?" He suggested that Facebook "change the algorithm so that people were more likely to see NYT, WSJ...over Daily Wire, Tomi Lahren, polarizing people." Flaherty was not subtle in his objective. "Intellectually my bias is to kick people off," he told the company executive.

In April 2021, Flaherty worked to strong-arm Google into ramping up its censorship operations. He told executives that his concerns were "shared at the highest (and I mean the highest) levels of the WH." There's "more work to be done," he instructed. He had the same talking points with Facebook that month, telling executives that he would have to explain to President Biden and Chief of Staff Ron Klain "why there is misinfo on the internet."

In nearly every case, the social media companies caved to the pressure of the White House.

Jenin Younes, litigation counsel at the New Civil Liberties Alliance, wrote in the *Wall Street Journal*:

"These emails establish a clear pattern: Mr. Flaherty, representing the White House, expresses anger at the companies' failure to censor Covid-related content to his satisfaction. The companies change their policies to address his demands. As a result, thousands of Americans were silenced for questioning government-approved Covid narratives."

The Biden administration's censorship operations ramped up in July 2021 as Americans realized that the Covid vaccines were not as effective as advertised. President Biden called publicly for social media companies to censor critics of Covid vaccines, telling the press that Big Tech was "killing people" by tolerating dissent. Biden later clarified that his comment was an attack on free speech, not tech CEOs. "My hope is that Facebook, instead of taking it personally that somehow I'm saying 'Facebook is killing people,' that they would do something about the misinformation," he explained.

Facebook heeded the call, and its employees updated the Biden White House the following week on their ramped-up censorship initiatives. A Facebook executive emailed government officials to say that they were working to censor pages that the administration found inconvenient. "I wanted to make sure you saw the steps we took just this past week to adjust policies on what we are removing with respect to misinformation, as well as steps taken to further address the 'disinfo dozen [vaccine critics including Robert F. Kennedy, Jr.].'" the executive wrote to the White House.

The following month, White House Covid Advisor Andy Slavitt successfully lobbied Twitter to remove journalist Alex Berenson from its platform after Berenson posted that the mRNA vaccines don't "stop infection. Or transmission." Berenson, who had his account reinstated following a lawsuit against Twitter, later uncovered emails that showed that Todd O'Boyle, a top Twitter lobbyist, circumvented company protocol to have junior Twitter employees ban his account. O'Boyle devised this pressure strategy through a coordinated campaign with White House advisor Andy Slavitt and Pfizer Board Member Scott Gottlieb.

Flaherty continued to spearhead the Biden White House's censorship efforts. "We are gravely concerned that your service is one of the top drivers of vaccine hesitancy—period," he wrote to a Facebook executive. "We want to know that you're trying, we want to know how we can help, and we want to know that you're not playing a shell game. . . .This would all be a lot easier if you would just be straight with us."

Of course, the mobster approach to free speech - *this would be a lot easier if you would just be straight with us, or else* - violates the First Amendment. Flaherty sought to control who could have a Facebook account, determine what they could post, and influence what they see. He didn't own the company or work for the CEO – he used the threat of government retribution to impose censorship.

Meta CEO Mark Zuckerberg later told Joe Rogan that "Biden administration officials used to call and scream at us demanding that we remove Covid related content, even things that were facts, or memes and humor…When we refused, we found ourselves under investigation by several agencies."

He continued:

> "During the Biden administration, when they were trying to roll out the vaccine program…while they were trying to push that program they also tried to censor anyone who is basically arguing against it. And they pushed us super hard to take down things that were honestly, were true. They basically pushed us and said, you know, that 'anything saying that says vaccines might have side effects, you basically need to take down.'"

That week, Zuckerberg released a statement admitting: "The only way that we can push back on this global trend is with the support of the US government. And that's why it's been so difficult over the past 4 years when even the US government has pushed for censorship. By going after us and other American companies, it has emboldened other governments to go even further." The confessions in January 2025 merely confirmed the strategy revealed through years of litigation and press leaks.

White House official Andy Slavitt joined Flaherty's efforts to crack down on dissent. In March 2021, he led the administration's unconstitutional crusade to prevent Americans from buying politically unfavorable books on Amazon. The effort, assisted by Flaherty, began on March 2, 2021, when Slavitt emailed the company demanding to speak to executives about the site's "high levels of propaganda and misinformation and disinformation."

The following month, Slavitt targeted Facebook, demanding that the company remove memes lampooning the Covid vaccine. In an April 2021 email, Nick Clegg, Facebook's president for global affairs, informed his team at Facebook that Slavitt, a Senior Advisor to President Biden, was "outraged . . that [Facebook] did not remove" a particular post.

When Clegg "countered that removing content like that would represent a significant incursion into traditional boundaries of free expression in the US," Slavitt disregarded the warning and the First Amendment, complaining that the posts "demonstrably inhibit[ed] confidence" in the Covid vaccines.

It is "axiomatic" under American law that the state cannot "induce, encourage, or promote" private companies to pursue unconstitutional aims. "Under the First Amendment there is no such thing as a false idea," the Supreme Court held in *Gertz v. Welch*. "However pernicious an opinion may seem, we depend for its correction not on the conscience of judges and juries, but on the competition of other ideas."

There is no *misinformation* carve-out to the First Amendment or pandemic exception to Constitutional Law, but the Biden administration, led by Flaherty, remains unremorseful for its leadership in the censorship apparatus.

In March 2023, Flaherty participated in an hour-long discussion at Georgetown University on his role in "how governments use social media to communicate with the public." An audience member asked Flaherty about his emails encouraging Facebook to censor private WhatsApp messages. "How do you justify legally telling a private messaging app what they can and cannot send?" Flaherty declined to answer. "I can't really comment on the specifics. I think the President has sort of made clear that one of the key parts of our Covid strategy is making sure the American people have access to reliable information as soon as they could get it, and, uh, you know, that's all part and parcel to that, but unfortunately I can't go too far into the litigation."

Three months later, Flaherty stepped down from his position at the White House. President Biden remarked, "The way Americans get their information is changing, and since Day 1, Rob has helped us meet people where they are." President Biden was right – Americans' access to information changed. The internet promised a liberating free exchange of ideas, but bureaucrats like Flaherty worked to implement informational tyranny. In Flaherty's words, this was all "part and parcel" to the White House strategy. On behalf of the administration, he demanded companies remove true content; he called on social media groups to remove journalists' accounts, suggested censoring citizens' private messages, and institutionalized the abuse of the First Amendment.

For his role in stifling Americans' access to information, the Democratic National Committee rewarded him by making him Deputy Campaign Manager for President Biden's (and later Kamala Harris's) 2024 presidential bids. Following President Trump's 2024 victory, Flaherty lamented that Elon Musk's purchase of Twitter and the popularity of independent podcasters contributed to his party "losing hold of culture;" a culture that he had dedicated his career to controlling for the benefit of his cabal.

The Security State Turns Inward

The censorship operations were not limited to select political-ly-appointed ideologues. The US Security State has been engaged in a decades-long war against free expression. At first, the targets appeared to be limited to transgressive cyber actors. Julian Assange and Edward Snowden looked like socially awkward hackers, not harbingers for what was to come. Following the 2001 terrorist attacks and Anthrax scare, the American Intelligence Community gained immense power through the PATRIOT Act and the creation of the Department of Homeland Security. But the powers designed to combat Islamic extremism developed into a weapon to purge domestic dissent. The leading government agency in the Covid response wasn't the CDC or the NIH; it was the Department of Homeland Security.

The censors adopted national security fear-mongering language to justify their assaults on civil liberties. The Biden administration's Department of Homeland Security described "misinformation" as a "terrorism threat to the United States." the DHS identified the informational terrorists as those who published information that would "undermine public trust in government institutions," specif-ically mentioning "false or misleading narratives" regarding Covid.

The encroachment of the U.S. Security State on the pillars of American society was suddenly a civilizational struggle in 2020. As the Covid regime overturned the Bill of Rights, the Security State shut down American society, eradicated due process, and captured the public health apparatus. This was not limited to

CIA bribes or FBI interference in the Hunter Biden laptop. The Cybersecurity and Infrastructure Security Agency (CISA), an agency within the DHS, took center stage in the Covid Coup.

On March 18, 2020 DHS replaced Health and Human Services as the Lead Federal Agency responding to Covid. FEMA, another DHS subsidiary, assumed control of vast swaths of government operations. CISA then hijacked the country's labor market and "cognitive infrastructure," a dystopian phrase for thoughts and opinions. That week, CISA divided the American workforce into categories of "essential" and "nonessential." Within hours, California became the first state to issue a "stay-at-home" edict. This began a previously unimaginable assault on Americans' civil liberties.

In *Missouri v. Biden*, the Fifth Circuit explained how CISA then transitioned to usurping the First Amendment. CISA held ongoing meetings with social media platforms to "push them to adopt more restrictive policies on censoring election-related speech." This broad category included everything relevant to an American voter, and the right to criticize lockdowns, vaccines, or the Hunter Biden laptop was suddenly subject to approval from the Department of Homeland Security.

Through a process known as "switchboarding," CISA officials dictated to Big Tech platforms what content was "true" or "false," which became Orwellian euphemisms for acceptable and prohibited speech. CISA's leaders reveled in their attacks on the First Amendment. They overturned hundreds of years of free speech protections, appointing themselves the arbiters of truth.

They were not subtle on this point. CISA Director Jen Easterly testified in *Missouri v. Biden*, "I think [it] is really, really dangerous if people get to pick their own facts." Instead, CISA would pick their facts and curate their newsfeeds for them. Easterly proudly claimed her agency concerned "cognitive infrastructure," meaning the thoughts in Americans' minds. CISA's Advisory Committee issued a 2022 Draft Report for Easterly that broadened "infrastructure" to include "the spread of false and misleading information because it poses a significant risk to critical function, like elections, public health, financial services and emergency responses."

The First Amendment presented an obstacle to their pursuit of thought control. Dr. Katie Starbird, a leader of CISA's censorship operations, lamented that Americans seemed to "accept malinformation as speech and within democratic norms." By "malinformation," Dr. Starbird meant true but politically inconvenient stories that emerged online. For example, CISA helped stifle a report on a Loudon County government official because "it was posted as part of a larger campaign to discredit the word of that official." There was nothing deceptive about the video, but it was part of a parents' group's opposition to Critical Race Theory, so CISA had the post removed. Similar stories emerged concerning reporting on vaccines, school closures, and lockdowns.

In 2024, America First Legal exposed more severe censorship directives from CISA and the Department of Homeland Security. According to internal documents, the Department of Homeland Security specifically targeted posts from Dr. Jay Bhattacharya that contradicted the government's inflated claims regarding the fatality rate of Covid. CISA then coordinated with left-wing censorship apparati like Media Matters, the Atlantic Council, and the Stanford Internet Observatory to suppress unapproved reports challenging the efficacy of masking, lockdowns, and vaccines. CISA determined that posts criticizing lockdown measures and mask mandates as consistent with "pro-Kremlin media." And they justified their censorship by claiming that "Anti-migrant, anti-Semitic, anti-Asian, racist, and xenophobic tropes have been at the forefront of Covid-19 related conspiracies."

Of course, the program explicitly violated the Constitution. The First Amendment does not discriminate based on the veracity of a statement. "Some false statements are inevitable if there is to be an open and vigorous expression of views in public and private conversation," the Supreme Court held in *United States v. Alvarez*. But CISA – led by zealots like Dr. Starbird – appointed themselves the arbiters of truth and worked with the most powerful information companies in the world to purge dissent.

CISA then launched nonprofits and non-governmental organizations (NGOs) that served as subsidiaries to continue their censorship. The government boasted that it "leveraged CISA's relationships with social media organizations to ensure priority treatment of misinformation reports." This process institutionalized the weaponization of information in direct defiance of the First Amendment.

In a draft copy of the Department of Homeland Security's "Quadrennial Homeland Security Review," the agency announced that CISA would target alleged mis- or mal-information on issues including the origins of Covid, the efficacy of Covid mRNA vaccines, racial justice, the United States' withdrawal from Afghanistan, and support for Ukraine. According to CISA Agent Brian Scully's testimony in *Missouri v. Biden*, Homeland Security coordinated its efforts with the CDC and the Intelligence Community.

In April 2022, the Department of Homeland Security announced the formation of the "Disinformation Governance Board," which was to be headed by Democratic activist Nina Jankowicz. According to Politico, Biden's Ministry of Truth was charged with "countering misinformation related to homeland security, focused specifically on irregular migration and Russia." Jankowicz was particularly familiar with disinformation - prior to her appointment, she was a staunch supporter of the Russiagate conspiracy and later worked to suppress coverage of Hunter Biden's laptop.

In 2022, as rumors circulated that Elon Musk was considering purchasing Twitter, Jankowicz told National Public Radio: "I shudder to think about if free speech absolutists were taking over more platforms." James Bovard responded in the *New York Post*: "That line is the Rosetta Stone for understanding the new Disinformation Governance Board. The goal is not 'truth' — which could arise from the clash of competing opinions. Instead, political overlords need power to exert pressure and pull to shape Americans' beliefs by discrediting, if not totally suppressing, disapproved opinions."

Fortunately, the absurdity of Jankowicz caused significant blowback from the public, as well as the news media, and the Biden administration was forced to scrap the Disinformation Governance Board later that year.

Other government agencies joined in the efforts. The National Science Foundation delivered grants to use artificial intelligence "track locations, people, and organizational affiliations of dubious COVID-19 information" based on whether they questioned CDC guidance. "That's not research, that's a government surveillance and censorship program laundered through academia," commented Andrew Lowenthal, CEO of liber-net, a digital civil liberties non-profit.

Lowenthal also reported that Meedan, one of Twitter's "anti-disinformation partners" during the Covid response, received U.S. Government funding to develop a program "called CryptoChat that advocated peering into private, encrypted messages to weed out 'misinformation.'" This grant was consistent with the aims of the White House and Rob Flaherty, who sought to impose government censorship on private WhatsApp messages.

The Security State's war against free expression continued until Judge Terry Doughty issued an injunction prohibiting the agency from colluding with Big Tech companies to censor Americans' speech. Doughty wrote: "The Free Speech Clause was enacted to prohibit just what [CISA] Director Easterly is wanting to do: allow the government to pick what is true and what is false."

Until Judge Doughty's injunction, the censors relied on anonymity to advance their agendas. Suzanne Spaulding, a member of CISA's "Misinformation & Disinformation Subcommittee," warned that it was "only a matter of time before someone realizes we exist and starts asking about our work." She was right, and the Plaintiffs in *Missouri v. Biden* brought their questions about CISA's work to the Fifth Circuit Court of Appeals. After initially wavering on the issue, the Court reinstated Judge Doughty's injunction against CISA. The Court held that CISA's switchboarding practice "likely coerced or significantly encouraged social-media platforms to moderate content...In doing so, the officials likely violated the First Amendment."

The Covid Regime, led by the Biden administration, responded with Orwellian doublethink: denying the censorship existed while arguing that it must continue. In a *Missouri v. Biden* hearing before the Fifth Circuit, the Biden Department of Justice argued that the allegations of censorship were merely "an assortment of out-of-context quotes and select portions of documents that distort the record to build a narrative that the bare facts simply do not support." Harvard Law Professor and former Biden advisor Larry Tribe called allegations of censorship a "thoroughly debunked conspiracy theory," in July 2023.

But as Orwell describes, the tyrants "hold simultaneously two opinions which cancel out, knowing them to be contradictory and believing in both of them." In its appeal of *Missouri v. Biden*, the government argued that stopping its censorship operations would cause "grave harm to the American people and our democratic processes." In court, DOJ attorneys defended the "efforts to reduce the spread of misinformation." Tribe echoed the DOJ's position that the censorship is both illusory and beneficial to society. Without social media censorship, Tribe argued, the United States will be "less secure as a nation" and its citizens will be subjected to a "cesspool of disinformation about election denialism and COVID." Put simply, the regime insisted the censorship didn't exist, and it was good that it did.

Public security has long been tyrants' excuse to criminalize free expression. Justice Oliver Wendell Holmes, Jr., compared handing out leaflets opposing World War I to "shouting fire in a crowded theater" in an opinion jailing President Wilson's political opponents. The Bush administration eroded civil liberties in the War on Terror through the false dichotomy that Americans were either "with us or with the terrorists." And the demands for obedience reached new heights in the Covid response, as safety from an invisible enemy was invoked to silence critics of the regime.

Just as the Supreme Court failed to uphold civil liberties following World War I, the Roberts Court was woefully derelict in its duty to protect the First Amendment rights of Americans in the Covid response.

In June 2024, the Supreme Court overturned the lower court's injunction in *Murthy v. Missouri* on the grounds that the plaintiffs lacked standing. The opinion, written by Justice Amy Coney Barrett, rested on omitted facts, skewed perceptions, and absurd conclusory statements. The dissent, issued by Justice Samuel Alito and joined by Justices Neil Gorsuch and Clarence Thomas, masterfully recounted the facts of the case and the inconsistency of the majority.

The majority opinion was bereft of references to the perpetrators of the censorship regime or their statements of coercion. Justice Barrett did not mention Rob Flaherty or Andy Slavitt – the two main henchmen behind the Biden administration's efforts – a single time in her holding. She did not address CISA or "switchboarding," nor did she discuss emails demonstrating the hijacking of social media companies. The dissent, however, devoted pages to recounting the White House's censorship crusade.

In dissent, Justice Alito cited how "the White House's emails were phrased virtually as orders and the officials' frequent follow-ups ensured that they were understood as such." Meta CEO Mark Zuckerberg later confirmed this finding in his confessions on Joe Rogan's podcast.

Within hours of taking office for his second term, however, President Trump took the action that the Roberts Court failed to do. On January 20, 2025, he signed an executive order "restoring freedom of speech and ending federal censorship," which declared it the policy of the United States to "secure the right of the American people to engage in constitutionally protected speech" and to "ensure that no Federal Government officer, employee, or agent engages in or facilitates any conduct that would unconstitutionally abridge the free speech of any American citizen."

Just three months earlier, John Kerry derided the "major block" of the First Amendment in a speech on climate change at the World Economic Forum. He lamented that the United States had insufficient resources to quash "disinformation" and called on his allies to "win the ground, win the right to govern" in order to be "free to be able to implement change." But with President Trump's initial actions against federal censorship, it appears that free speech has won the ground and the right to govern. It remains to be seen how the Intelligence Community, CISA, and other actors will respond.

Censoring the Doctors

While the Intelligence Community and the federal bureaucracy worked behind the scenes to quash dissent in the public sphere, California took the next logical step in the censorship crusade by banning non-approved Covid narratives from the medical profession.

California Governor Gavin Newsom signed Assembly Bill 2098 into law in September 2022 after the state legislature passed the measure without holding public discussion or debate. The law authorized the California Medical Board to punish doctors who shared Covid "misinformation," defined as any statement that "is contradicted by contemporary scientific consensus."

The law targeted three categories of Covid-related speech. First, it threatened doctors who deviated from orthodoxy on the nature of the virus, including the danger it posed to healthy young adults. Second, it regulated how doctors could treat patients. Third, it focused on controlling medical narratives surrounding mask mandates and mRNA shots. The legislative record revealed that its proponents hoped to address the "problem" of doctors who "call into question public health efforts such as masking and vaccination." Their proposed solution was to end the debate in the professional sphere.

The law's broad definition of "misinformation," subject to change at any moment based on the capricious whims of bureaucrats, was a deliberate attack on free speech. It stood athwart two centuries of First Amendment jurisprudence and American tradition. "If there is any fixed star in our constitutional constellation, it is that no official, high or petty, can prescribe what shall be orthodox in politics, nationalism, religion, or other matters of opinion or force citizens to confess by word or act their faith therein," the Supreme Court held in 1943. Under the façade of "public health," censors sought to overturn the core foundation of American free speech.

Jacob Sullum explained in the *New York Post*:

> "The new law... makes physicians subject to discipline for sharing their honest opinions regarding COVID-19 if the medical board thinks they deviate from the 'scientific consensus,' a term the law does not define. That nebulous standard poses a due process problem, since the law does not give doctors fair notice of which conduct it reaches. It also poses a free speech problem, since it encourages self-censorship."

The bill's primary author was State Senator Richard Pan, a Democrat doctor from Sacramento with a longstanding disregard for the First Amendment. Though he appears to be little more than an empty vessel steered toward political opportunism, Dr. Pan is the archetype of the Covid authoritarians. While Americans surrendered to lockdowns and mandates, he demonstrated an ongoing disdain for constitutional freedoms and disregard for human suffering.

He spouted untruths while accusing his opponents of *misinformation*, and he used the cudgel of "public health" to justify his attacks on the American way of life. All the while, he appeared obtuse to the profound damage his policies had on children and championed the fundamental tenets of the Covid regime: censorship, lockdowns, school closures, mask mania, vaccine mandates, and a corrupt relationship with the pharmaceutical industry.

In an op-ed for the *Washington Post*, he called the anti-vaccine movement "akin to domestic terrorism," and demanded social media companies ban users and groups that challenged government-approved Covid narratives. Pan accused vaccine skeptics of having "a financial interest" in their initiatives but notably ignored his own potential conflicts of interest, as he received more campaign contributions from the pharmaceutical industry than any other California state representative after he introduced legislation to heighten vaccine requirements. Pan is less critical of his own misinformation; he has insisted that "puberty blockers" are "reversible" and that "natural immunity is clearly rubbish."

When Governor Newsom signed Dr. Pan's censorship regime into law, free speech advocates warned that punishing doctors who challenged "contemporary scientific consensus" jeopardized the scientific method and ran afoul of the First Amendment. The Liberty Justice Center explained:

"The scientific consensus has been evolving throughout the COVID-19 pandemic. The Centers for Disease Control and other public health authorities have constantly shifted their public presentation of scientific data. At the beginning of the pandemic, health authorities insisted the public not wear masks, then soon reversed that decision. Governor Newsom himself closed schools and even outdoor spaces— policies now widely acknowledged as unscientific and harmful."

California doctors objected to the Newsom-Pan Ministry of Truth and filed suit. In court, they argued that the facts indicated that the "true goal of AB 2098" was to "suppress unpopular ideas or information," in stark violation of the First Amendment. They continued, "there could hardly be a clearer example of a viewpoint-discriminatory law, because AB 2098 privileges speech that is consistent with the 'scientific consensus' (however ill-defined that phrase may be) and punishes speech that diverges from it."

In January 2023, U.S. District Judge William Shubb issued a preliminary injunction that prevented the law from taking effect, holding that the law was "unconstitutionally vague." Shubb continued, "COVID-19 is a quickly evolving area of science that in many aspects eludes consensus." Greg Dolin, a lawyer for the plaintiffs, agreed. "This Act is a blatant attempt to silence doctors whose views, though based on thorough scientific research, deviate from the government-approved 'party line,'" he said after the release of the injunction. "At no point has the State of California been able to articulate the line between permissible and impermissible speech."

In October 2023, California Democrats quietly repealed A.B. 2098 as coronamania waned and the courts refuted the attack on First Amendment rights. The Ninth Circuit Court of Appeals dismissed challenges to the law as moot after Governor Newsom's efforts to silence dissident doctors failed under judicial review.

. . .

The campaign against free speech in California was representative of the censorious cabal that took power in 2020. The perpetrators spread widely debunked falsehoods and threatened to ruin the careers of those who dissented. They weaponized the state against their political opponents and assumed their self-appointed moral authority transcended any legal limitation to their powers. The attack on our First Amendment was deliberate, and it was launched by those who sought to acquire political authority and shield personal liability.

From the outset, the Covid censors' focus was self-interest, not public health. They smeared their critics as anti-science, pro-Kremlin, grandma-killing racists who drank bleach and ate horse dewormer. Their incompetence and wrongdoing hid behind their shameless impatience for dissent.

Anthony Fauci infamously remarked, "Attacks on me, quite frankly, are attacks on science." White House Press Secretary Jen Psaki blamed vaccine hesitancy on "Russian disinformation efforts" which she vowed to "fight with every tool we have." Justin Trudeau said of the unvaccinated: "They are extremists who don't believe in science, they're often misogynists, also often racists." CNN and the FDA referred to ivermectin as "horse dewormer," deliberately omitting that the drug's inventors received a 2015 Nobel Prize for its use in humans.

The censors claimed that their critics were so irredeemable that they should be stripped of their most basic rights as citizens. Covid law and the regime's infallible leaders denied dissidents their First Amendment freedoms. All the while, the censors replaced free speech with carefully calculated *misinformation* concerning the virus, vaccines, masks, natural immunity, and lockdowns. While public officials touted party lines to a sycophantic press corps, a more insidious censorship operation worked to eradicate dissent from the marketplace of ideas. As Judge Terry Doughty wrote, Covid censorship sparked arguably "the most massive attack against free speech in United States' history."

THE QUIET COUP: LOCKDOWNS
AND THE RIGHT TO TRAVEL

66"Restricting citizens' ability to travel is a hallmark of a police state," legal scholar Eugene Kontorovich asserted in 2021. "Infectious disease will always be with us. It cannot become an excuse to give the federal government carte blanche to control the lives of citizens." Yet the American government pursued that *carte blanche* in blatant disregard of the country's long-standing right to travel. Executive orders put citizens under house arrest as the disease became the pretext for usurping the most basic human liberty. Governors boasted of jailing their residents for strolling outside, the Intelligence Community imposed arbitrary dictates on who could continue work, children sat indoors for months on end, and the elderly died alone.

Beginning on March 16, 2020, nearly every state imposed "stay-at-home" orders, threatening jail time for the non-compliant. Local officials called on police to round up those who violated their decrees, and they demanded that local law enforcement monitor family gatherings. This totalitarianism was not reserved for brash political celebrities like Andrew Cuomo or

Gavin Newsom. Supposedly moderate figures like Maryland's Larry Hogan unleashed their authoritarian impulses.

These efforts clearly violated Americans' freedoms. Since the Civil War, the Supreme Court upheld the right to travel as a constitutional liberty inextricable from the Thirteenth Amendment's prohibition of slavery. "The right to travel is part of the 'liberty' of which the citizen cannot be deprived without due process of law under the Fifth Amendment," the Supreme Court held in 1958. "Freedom of movement is basic in our scheme of values."

President Franklin D. Roosevelt's internment of Japanese-Americans during World War II remains the most notable violation of the right since 1865. Though *Korematsu v. United States* (1944) upheld FDR's Executive Order 9066, the decision later joined *Plessy v. Ferguson* and *Dred Scott* in the "anti-canon" of American jurisprudence. Chief Justice Roberts wrote in 2018, "*Korematsu* was gravely wrong the day it was decided, has been overruled in the court of history and - to be clear – has no place in law under the Constitution."

But everything changed on March 19, 2020, when California became the first state to issue a stay-at-home" order. It overturned centuries of Anglo-American law and epidemiological practice and unveiled the implementation of a police state that the United States had long resisted.

An Unprecedented Response

From the American Revolution to 2020, pandemics and epidemics affected every major American city without the government overturning the right to travel. Smallpox halted the Continental Army from taking Quebec in 1775. John Adams wrote to his wife, "The smallpox is ten times more terrible than Britons, Canadians, and Indians, together." An unusually rainy summer in 1780 led to a breakout of malaria for soldiers in Virginia. "Disease, particularly malaria, reduced British fighting capacity more effectively than patriot bullets," writes historian Peter McCandless. Yellow fever struck Philadelphia in 1793 and killed ten percent of the city's population. All precautions were voluntary, and there were no efforts to quarantine the healthy population.

Intercontinental migration led to a series of cholera pandemics in the 19th century, and the resulting government sanitation efforts coined the term "public health." Spanish flu reached the United States following World War I and killed approximately 675,000 Americans.

After the advent of antibiotics, epidemics continued with far less fatal results. In 1949, polio spread rapidly through the United States. By 1952, there were 57,000 reported cases, resulting in 3,000 deaths and over 20,000 cases of paralysis. Jeffrey Tucker writes in *Liberty or Lockdown*:

> "Though there was no cure, and no vaccine, there was a long incubation period before symptoms would reveal themselves, and while there was a great deal of confusion about how it was transmitted, the thought of locking down an entire state, nation, or world was inconceivable. The concept of a universal 'shelter in place' order was nowhere imaginable. Efforts to impose 'social distancing' were selective and voluntary."

In 1957, the Asian flu arrived in the United States. It killed over one million people globally and was particularly devastating for the elderly and those with comorbidities. The *New York Times* cautioned, "Let us all keep a cool head about Asian influenza as the statistics on the spread and the virulence of the disease begin to accumulate."

And the nation kept a cool head. Localities protected the vulnerable, but the Eisenhower administration never demanded submission from the citizenry. Public health initiatives remained isolated, voluntary, and temporary. There were no widespread edicts of lockdowns or house arrest. The government did not coerce healthy people into their homes or shutter businesses. Police did not criminalize free movement or institute curfews. Governors did not order law enforcement to shut down holiday gatherings, nor did they threaten citizens with jail time if they violated stay-at-home orders.

The Court's 1958 decision upholding the "right to travel freely" came just months after the 1957 flu pandemic and less than a decade after the polio epidemic. For nearly 250 years, the United States resisted the "hallmark of a police state," maintaining the right to travel despite public health threats related to influenza, cholera, smallpox, and more.

"Freedom of movement" remained basic in the nation's "scheme of values" until the public health apparatus and American political leaders overthrew precedent in March 2020. Divorced from the constraints of the past, politicians and bureaucrats rejoiced in their *carte blanche* to control the lives of citizens. Tyrannical house arrest orders became commonplace, and constitutional liberty disappeared from the Republic.

The House Arrests of 2020

After Trump's March 16 press conference, freedom of movement was no longer "basic in the nation's scheme of values." Longstanding legal precedent was suddenly abandoned, as was the accumulated wisdom of lessons from centuries of pandemic responses.

Three days later, CISA divided the country into essential and nonessential categories, permitting liberty for media, technology, and large commercial facilities but imposing tyranny for less favorable groups like bars, restaurants, churches, and gyms. Hours after the release of CISA's memo, California became the first state to issue a "stay-at-home" order. Governor Newsom decreed, "I order all individuals living in the State of California to stay home or at their place of residence except as needed to maintain continuity of operations of the federal critical infrastructure sectors."

Tyranny engulfed the Golden State. Law enforcement promptly criminalized exercising basic human liberties. "The days of trying to get voluntary compliance are really over," San Diego County Sheriff Bill Gore said in April 2020. "The message is going to go out to all of public safety here in the county that we will start issuing citations for violations of the public order and the governor's executive order."

A survey of anecdotes from 2020 reveal the total abolition of liberty in California; police handcuffed citizens surfing alone. Santa Monica threatened to fine anyone who walked outside to the pier. A paddle boarder faced six months in jail for entering the Pacific Ocean. Los Angeles police arrested residents for attending "super-spreader events."

Newsom was not alone in his capricious fiats. In New Jersey, police charged parents with "child endangerment" for bringing their children to a social gathering, fined brides and grooms for having weddings, and arrested a man for leading an outdoor exercise class. In Maryland, Republican Governor Larry Hogan threatened people with one year in jail if they violated his stay-at-home orders. Hogan's police force arrested those who did not provide a "valid reason" for leaving their homes. Hawaii created "checkpoints" to arrest and fine people who violated the state's stay-at-home order. Rhode Island police charged men from

Massachusetts for driving into the state to play golf. Delaware police arrested 12 people for violating the state's "emergency gathering ordinance" limiting meetings to 10 people. Connecticut arrested restaurant owners for permitting dancing. Idaho police arrested a woman for walking in a public park and detained a mother for taking her children to the playground. Across the country, leaders chained off playgrounds, arrested groups sitting outside, poured sand in skateparks, cut down basketball hoops, and criminalized protest.

In Colorado, a former police officer was arrested and handcuffed for having a softball catch with his six-year-old daughter at an empty baseball field. The father reflected on what the incident meant to his daughter. "She's learned that our constitutional rights are something worth standing up for," he said. "She got to witness a violation of civil rights."

While the arrests may seem like isolated incidents, they were part of a widespread authoritarian campaign to demand submission from citizens. They were the force behind a broader message to the public: *Submit to power, don't ask questions, don't leave the house. Watch Netflix, cash your stimulus check, don't resist. Stay inside. Save Lives. Tune in. Shut up. Lock down.*

Lockdowns stripped Americans of their First Amendment rights to assemble and protest. In Hawaii, the Honolulu Police Department issued criminal citations against lockdown protestors for violating GovernorDavid Ige's prohibition on public gatherings. In North Carolina, masked policeman arrested the leader of "Reopen NC" for violating the "stay-at-home order."

"I feel my rights have been completely removed," one protestor in North Carolina remarked. "The world I'm raising my children in has been completely changed."

In Cincinnati, Ohio police arrested a 25-year-old man for going outdoors (in violation of the governor's stay-at-home order) and posting a video on Instagram saying "We don't give a [expletive] about coronavirus." In North Carolina, police arrested abortion protestors for gathering outdoors in violation of state decrees.

Maryland, nicknamed "The Free State" for its opposition to the Prohibition movement, quickly turned to despotism. Larry Hogan, the rotund Republican governor, issued strict stay-at-home orders and encouraged police to arrest those who exercised their right to free movement. When the press asked about reports of Marylanders arrested for violating lockdown orders, Hogan responded, "It sends a great message," The *message* was clear: comply or be jailed. "We're not playing around," he added.

In Michigan, Gretchen Whitmer banned fishing and criminalized driving cars to unapproved destinations. Her state police arrested restaurant owners for not shutting down their businesses and jailed those who defied her orders. "The goal here is simple: Stay Home," she explained.

The house arrest in Michigan divided state law enforcement. "What's the definition of an arrest? It's basically taking away your free will, your right to move about," said Michigan County Sheriff Dar Leaf in May 2020. "And an unlawful arrest is when you do it unlawfully, so when you are ordered to your home, are you under arrest? Yeah, by definition you are."

In April, Detroit police issued 730 citations and 1,000 warnings to citizens who violated Whitmer's house arrest orders. Whitmer's political allies, including the State Attorney General, supported her suppression of liberty, but others maintained their objections.

Four sheriffs from northern Michigan released a statement claiming that Whitmer was "overstepping her executive authority" with unconstitutional orders. "We will deal with every case as an individual situation and apply common sense in assessing the apparent violation," they said in a joint press release. "Each of us took an oath to uphold and defend the Michigan Constitution, as well as the US Constitution, and to ensure that your God given rights are not violated. We believe that we are the last line of defense in protecting your civil liberties."

The restrictions on the right to travel continued through the year. Fauci and the CDC warned Americans not to travel for Thanksgiving. Governor Cuomo banned New Yorkers from having more than ten people at their holiday meals. He insisted that law enforcement charge families and friends who violated his arbitrary limit. Some police, however, were not comfortable with following this directive. They complained that it was unconstitutional, and they worried how citizens would react to the State imposing its decree in their dining rooms. "We will not be peeking in your windows or attempting to enter your property to count the number of persons at your table on Thanksgiving," one sheriff assured residents.

Cuomo was enraged. He called sheriffs' hesitation to enforce his executive fiat "frightening to democracy." He attacked their loyalty to the state and their right to challenge his authority in exerting lockdowns on New Yorkers. "It's arrogant," he insisted. "It violates [their] constitutional duty."

Arrogant, unconstitutional, and frightening to democracy. Before 2020, that is how Americans would describe a petty tyrant seeking to criminalize family gatherings. But all that changed in March, and Cuomo became a media sensation for his authoritarian response to the virus.

Sheriffs insisted that entering homes to count the number of grandmothers and cousins sharing dessert would be unlawful. "We are regulated by the legal guidelines of our response to complaints as to whether or not we have license and privilege to enter private residences, based upon warrant, consent or exigent circumstances," Steuben County Sheriff James Allard said in a statement.

Cuomo, who won a 2020 Emmy Award for his Covid television appearances, adjusted his script in addressing the electorate. He told the public that they should express their love by making their family members spend the holidays alone. "My personal advice is you don't have family gatherings – even for Thanksgiving," he told reporters. "If you love someone, it is better and safer to stay away." Cuomo then announced that he would host his mother and daughters for Thanksgiving dinner, though he cancelled his plans amid public backlash.

Many states, including neighboring New Jersey and Connecticut, adopted similar guidelines for the holiday, but the public health apparatus was unsatisfied. " We know people may have made mistakes over the Thanksgiving time period," White House Coronavirus Response Coordinator Deborah Birx said in early December. She lectured those who "gathered" with others over the holiday, "you need to assume you're infected." This attitude ushered in a new wave of Covid edicts going into Christmas 2020.

In the end, the policies were a public health failure. They failed to stop the spread of Covid, and excess deaths unrelated to the coronavirus skyrocketed. One study estimated that the United States lockdown measures saved a total of 4,000 lives, approximately ten percent of the number of Americans who die annually from the flu. In contrast, there were 100,000 non-Covid "excess deaths" per year in 2020 and 2021 according to the CDC. Young adult deaths ran 27% above historical trends due to increased accidents, overdoses, and homicides.

After declining in 2018 and 2019, the youth suicide rate soared in 2020 and 2021. Homicides increased 56% in Americans aged

10 to 14 and 44% in ages 15 to 19. Meanwhile, the majority of Covid deaths occurred in Americans who were already above the age of life expectancy.

The lockdown efforts weren't just futile – they were devastating and counterproductive. A 2023 study from three Johns Hopkins researchers found: "The science of lockdowns is clear, the data are in: the lives saved were a drop in the bucket compared to the staggering collateral costs imposed." Governors and bureaucrats eviscerated human liberty in the lockdowns, and they are responsible for hundreds of thousands of untimely deaths.

Understanding this didn't require the benefit of hindsight. Supreme Court precedent was unambiguous in defending citizens' constitutional right to travel. For 200 years, the government maintained American liberty despite a vast array of public health initiatives.

Further, there was ample medical literature warning against lockdowns before March 2020. In 2019, the WHO warned that lockdowns were ineffective and inadvisable. In January 2020, Dr. Howard Markel wrote in the *Washington Post* that house arrest and mass quarantine would not contain the disease and would have significant societal ramifications. Ten days before California's first stay-at-home order, 800 public health scientists warned against lockdowns and quarantines in an open letter.

In April 2020, a study revealed that "full lockdown policies in Western Europe countries have no evidence impacts on the Covid-19 epidemic." Scientist Mark Changizi wrote at the time, "Lockdowns were NOT common sense measures. They were hysterical reactions out of fear."

"Almost no awareness of the impact on civil rights, as if emergency declaration, suspension of rights, house arrest, mass unemployment and business shutdowns is just something democratic governments sometimes do," he continued. "There was no historical precedent for putting the entire healthy population in 'quarantine.'" The following month, a study found that stay-at-home orders would "destroy at least seven times more years of human life" than they would save.

It turned out the "scientific basis" for social distancing stemmed from Laura Glass, a fourteen-year-old girl from New Mexico who submitted a school project that argued that separating the population was as effective as a vaccine. But outside of the junior high science fair, the experiment was a disaster.

By September 2020, the failures of lockdowns were readily apparent, but many states stayed their course. Donald Luskin wrote in the *Wall Street Journal*, "Six months into the Covid-19 pandemic, the US has now carried out two large-scale experiments in public health." He explained:

> "First, in March and April, the lockdown of the economy to arrest the spread of the virus, and second, since mid-April, the reopening of the economy. The results are in. Counter-intuitive though it may be, statistical analysis shows that locking down the economy didn't contain the disease's spread and reopening it didn't unleash a second wave of infections."

While the most vulnerable suffered, the powerful prospered. Politicians gained unprecedented authority over their citizens. Multinational companies like consulting giant McKinsey received lucrative government contracts to implement tyranny. In the first 100 days of the pandemic, McKinsey amassed more than $100 million in contracts to advise local, state, and federal officials in their response to the virus. *Politico* reported that Jared Kushner brought in a "suite of McKinsey consultants" to take "charge of the most important challenges facing the federal government" in March 2020.

California doled out tens of millions of dollars in no-bid contracts to McKinsey during the pandemic, as did Illinois, Massachusetts, Ohio, New Jersey, New York, Virginia, Atlanta, Chicago, Los Angeles, New Orleans, and St. Louis. In July 2020, *ProPublica* wrote: "For the world's best-known corporate-management consultants, helping tackle the pandemic has been a bonanza. It's not clear what the government has gotten in return."

The laptop class of consultants and bureaucrats grew immensely rich while they augmented their power. The Covid regime siphoned Americans' tax dollars to profiteers who implemented tyranny and the ensuing destruction. Those who reaped the benefits had the luxury of remaining detached from the costs. The cronyism ushered in a previously unimaginable despotism.

Aspects of lockdowns continued into 2021, and the obstinate Covid regime continued its abolition of freedom. Those responsible for the policies – including Debi Birx, Anthony Fauci, Joe Biden, and Donald Trump – refuse to admit error. Instead, they regret not implementing more tyrannical measures.

Doubling Down – "Go Medieval On It"

"I wish when we went into lockdown, we looked like Italy," Dr. Deborah Birx told television cameras in August 2020, standing outside in a mask. "People weren't allowed out of their houses, and they couldn't come out but once every two weeks to buy groceries... [they] had to have a certificate that said they were allowed."

Despite the arrests, the school closures, and the abolition of liberty, American leaders lamented their failure to implement greater tyranny. Birx regretted that Americans had been permitted to go to the grocery store more than once every fourteen days, the timespan she insisted would help *flatten the curve.*

In her memoir, she later boasted that she censored Dr. Scott Atlas, the only member of the Trump Administration resisting lockdowns. She worked with the White House Communications team to block him from media appearances and sought to kick him off the Covid task force.

The Covid regime shared Birx's views that response to the virus had not been sufficiently autocratic. Peter Walker, a longtime senior partner at McKinsey, insisted that the Chinese deserved "high praise" for their response to the virus. In April 2020, he appeared on Fox News and argued: "I think the harsh action that they took, given the scale of China and the number of big cities...was exactly what they needed to do to be able to prevent the outbreak from going any further."

Host Tucker Carlson responded, "What would you say to the families of those who died, starved to death alone in their apartments, or the people who are wondering where their relatives went after they were bundled into Chinese police vans?" Walker conceded that every death was "heartbreaking" but applauded China's efforts to combat the virus. Like Birx, he said the more despotic responses were preferable to the United States' less stringent lockdowns, which he called a "late start."

Jerome Adams, President Trump's Surgeon General, had similar reflections in 2022. "We NEVER locked down," he tweeted. When critics responded with articles from 2020 outlining lockdown orders, Adams fired back, "Did we lock down like China?" Like Birx, he insisted that a proper lockdown would have required even less freedom.

In August 2023, Adams wrote that lockdowns and face masks were "unequivocally effective," posting an article that featured

666666666

4444444444

masked citizens behind the caption: "CORONAVIRUS: STAY HOME, SAVE LIVES. ACT LIKE YOU'VE GOT IT. ANYONE CAN SPREAD IT." He now argues that the lockdowns were effective, but they also should have been stricter.

Dr. Fauci has expressed those beliefs as well. In October 2022, he defended his decision to lock down the country, saying that he helped "save lives." He regretted that the efforts were not more stringent, saying that the government should have been "much more strict in demanding mask wearing."

This was consistent with Fauci's previous statements. In August 2020, Fauci co-authored an article for *Cell*. "America's Doctor" envisioned permanent human separation, a process that could only be achieved through a system of tyranny even grander than Covid response.

"The ongoing COVID-19 pandemic reminds us that over-crowding in dwellings and places of human congregation…as well as human geographic movement catalyzes disease spread," Fauci wrote. "Living in greater harmony with nature will require changes in human behavior as well as other radical changes that may take decades to achieve: rebuilding the infrastructures of human existence."

Radical changes that may take decades to achieve: rebuilding the infrastructure of human existence. "Rebuilding" tacitly acknowledged that the public health apparatus had destroyed the existing infrastructure. They had bulldozed constitutional liberties and societal norms.

New York Times writer Donald G. McNeil, a frequent correspondent of Fauci's, urged the country to adopt unconstitutional tyranny in his column from February 28, 2020: "To Take on the Coronavirus, Go Medieval on It." He wrote, "The medieval way, inherited from the era of the Black Death, is brutal: Close the borders, quarantine the ships, pen terrified citizens up inside their poisoned cities."

Pen terrified citizens up inside their poisoned cities. This was not mere posturing. McNeil wanted the country to implement Eastern-style tyranny to combat Covid. In private email exchanges with Fauci, he confirmed his animosity toward individual rights, calling Americans "selfish pigs" while glorifying the authoritarian response and widespread submission in Xi's China.

"A lot of average Chinese behaved incredibly heroically in the face of the virus," McNeil emailed Fauci. "Meanwhile, in America, people tend to act like selfish pigs interested only in saving themselves." Fauci responded, "You make some very good points, Donald." McNeil later wrote in the *New York Post*, "we must have ways to stop and even imprison doctors who prescribe false cures."

In October 2020, Fauci bragged to an audience that the country had gone Medieval in its response. "I recommended to the president that we shut the country down." Like McNeil, he lamented that the United States had not implemented more totalitarian measures like China. "Unfortunately, since we actually did not shut down completely, the way China did, the way Korea did, the way Taiwan did, we actually did see spread even though we shut down," he explained, though he did not address the other countries' ongoing Covid infections.

Fauci appears callously indifferent to the costs of implementing *radical changes* to *rebuild the infrastructure of human existence.* In April 2021, "America's Doctor" appeared before a Congressional subcommittee wearing a mask. "Fifteen days to slow the spread turned into one year of lost liberty," Rep. Jim Jordan said before asking Fauci: "What metrics, what measures, what has to happen before Americans get more freedoms?"

Fauci replied, "I don't look at this as a liberty thing." Those concerns – including Americans' Constitutional rights - were less important than his grand initiative to *rebuild human existence*. The previous year, he admitted that lockdowns may be "inconvenient" for Americans and that he had not weighed the costs and benefits of closing schools.

Georgetown University hired Dr. Fauci in 2023 and hosted him for a forum on the Covid response. Fauci issued unequivocal support for lockdowns, calling them "absolutely justified." He then suggested that lockdowns could be used to implement mandatory vaccination campaigns. "If you have a vaccine available, you might want to lock down temporarily so you can get everybody vaccinated," he explained.

Fauci was not subtle about his ambitious initiatives. By *radical change*, he meant abolishing centuries of Anglo-American legal tradition and personal liberties. The only means of implementing his plan to *rebuild the infrastructure of human existence* would be totalitarian control far beyond the constraints of the US Constitution.

Make America Medieval Again

Though the media enjoyed portraying them as foil characters, President Trump and Dr. Fauci have largely agreed on the decision to lock down the country. Through the 2020 and 2024 elections, President Trump repeatedly defended the lockdowns that he implemented.

On March 29, 2020, the national mitigation plan for Covid was set to expire. "Fifteen days to stop the spread" had run its course, and President Trump addressed the nation from the Rose Garden. He announced that the lockdowns would extend another month. Despite the demonstrated failure from the first two weeks, the Trump administration began the process of moving goalposts that deprived Americans of liberty until the Covid emergency officially ended on May 11, 2023.

Trump campaigned on his decision to lock down the country in 2020. From March to Election Day, he repeatedly told crowds that following Fauci's orders had been the "right thing to do." On March 24, the Trump re-election campaign posted a video of Fauci bragging that Trump never stood against his lockdown dogma. "The president has listened to what I have said," Fauci said. "When I've made recommendations, he's taken them. He's never countered or overridden me."

In April, Trump told reporters that he controlled the nation's ability to reopen. "The president of the United States calls the shots," he said at a news briefing. "They can't do anything without the approval of the president of the United States." He admitted that he chose to lock down the nation despite having alternative options. "I could have kept it open. I thought of keeping it open," he went on. "We've done this right."

Fauci again told reporters that Trump had implemented his recommendations. Trump later gushed over Fauci, "I like him. I think he is terrific." Trump took full responsibility for the lockdowns that month tweeting, "For the purpose of creating conflict and confusion, some in the Fake News Media are saying that it is the Governors decision to open up the states, not that of the President of the United States & the Federal Government. Let it be fully understood that this is incorrect... It is the decision of the President, and for many good reasons."

In September, Trump defended Birx and Fauci as a "group of very smart people" who convinced him to lock down the country. "We closed up...a group of very smart people walk in and say, 'Sir, we have to close it.' And we did the right thing. We closed it." Later that month, he continued his boasts at a campaign rally in Pennsylvania: "We did the right thing. We closed the country down."

He continued his messaging until Election Day. In October, Trump opened the presidential debate by insisting that his lockdowns had saved millions of lives. "I closed up the greatest economy in the world in order to fight this horrible disease that came from China," he remarked. He campaigned in Arizona the next week bragging, "We did just the right thing. We closed it down." On November 1, he told a crowd in Georgia, "I had to shut it down. And we did the right thing. We shut it down."

After the 2020 election, Trump's White House continued to push for lockdown measures. In December 2020, Trump called on Florida to implement mask mandates, close restaurants, and demand strict social distancing. When Governor DeSantis refused to follow those suggestions, the White House sent follow-up demands in January 2021 during the last ten days of Trump's first term. The Trump administration called for "aggressive mitigation," including "uniform implementation of effective face masking (two or three ply and well-fitting) and strict physical distancing."

The rift between Trump and DeSantis continued in the 2024 presidential election. In May 2023, Trump attacked DeSantis for the decision to reopen Florida. Trump wrote that New York Governor Andrew Cuomo "did better" on the Covid response than DeSantis by locking down the state. Cuomo relished the compliment, tweeting "Donald Trump tells the truth, finally." Trump's statement was far from accurate; the CDC reported that New York's age-adjusted deaths were 23% higher than Florida's.

An April 2022 study found that New York had the third-worst Covid response when measured by economy, education, and mortality. Florida ranked sixth best. Cuomo's response led to the fourth-worst mortality rate in the nation despite his dictatorial orders.

Trump's 2024 campaign also found an unlikely ally in California Governor Gavin Newsom. In a Fox News interview, Trump touted that he "used to get along great" with Newsom. "He was always very nice to me. Said the greatest things," he added. Newsom echoed the sentiment, boasting that he had an "incredible relationship" with Trump when they worked to lock down the nation. In notable contrast, Florida maintained lower cumulative all-cause age-adjusted excess mortality than California throughout the entire pandemic.

Trump's position on lockdowns is now clear. "The one thing I have never been credited for is the job we did on Covid," he told Fox News in January 2024. He sided with the two most ardent defenders of destroying American liberty against the governor who drew the most controversy for reopening his state. In June 2023, Trump gave a definitive answer when Bret Baier asked if he had "any regrets" on how his administration handled Covid. "No," he said, shaking his head. Two months later, he told Glenn Beck, "We did a great job with Covid – has never been acknowledged, but it will be in history."

"A Virtually Unconditional Personal Right"

None of the presidential advisors from March 2020 – including Birx, Fauci, and Kushner – have expressed remorse or regret for putting Americans under house arrest. In the 1,141 days of the Covid state of emergency, Americans lost their foundational liberty to move freely; it was a blatant usurpation of the United States' constitutional tradition.

In 1941, Justice Robert Jackson wrote that Americans have the right to interstate travel "either for temporary sojourn or for the establishment of permanent residence." Citing the Constitution's Privileges and Immunities Clause, he wrote, "if national citizenship means less than this, it means nothing." For Americans passing through Maryland under Larry Hogan, national citizenship ended up meaning nothing.

Over fifty years later, the Court held in *Saenz v. Roe*, "The word 'travel' is not found in the text of the Constitution. Yet the 'constitutional right to travel from one State to another' is firmly embedded in our jurisprudence." This right disappeared for New York parents who wanted to bring their children to a gathering with classmates from New Jersey.

In 1969, Justice Potter Stewart called the right to travel "a virtually unconditional personal right, guaranteed by the Constitution to us all." Yet, in states across the country, governors instituted a police state. The Covid regime went "medieval" in its response, *penning terrified citizens up inside their poisoned cities* as Fauci and McNeil advocated.

Americans lost the basic liberty to move unencumbered in their country. Government officials implemented tyranny without any mention of due process. They are worse than unremorseful; they lament their inability to enact greater despotism.

While anecdotes like golfing arrests and fines for children's playdates may seem trivial compared to the vast array of Covid mandates, they represent the coordinated effort to punish individuals for exercising their right to travel freely. The downstream consequences of this tyranny were monumental. It overturned the right to protest, destroyed years of human life, unwound the social fabric, and permanently damaged a generation of young Americans.

RELIGIOUS FREEDOM

The consequences of lockdowns were not limited to freedom of movement or assembly. Once leaders had the green light to shutter large swaths of society, they wielded that power to impose their newly established ideology.

A new creed emerged in 2020 that divided society into true believers and heretics. Its adherents donned face coverings and regularly engaged in emotional self-flagellation. They put their faith in pharmaceutical products and unrelentingly sought to convert their neighbors. Those who questioned their dogma were cast aside as irredeemable. Just as the *New York Times* suggested the country "go medieval" on the coronavirus, society returned to a Dark Age persecution of iconoclasts.

The central powers banished dissidents while the United States' capital city declared a holiday for its beatified leader. In Washington, DC, the Mayor renamed Christmas Eve "Dr. Anthony S. Fauci Day" in 2020. Mass media and cultural madness ushered in the nascent faith. Rev. John Naugle later observed, "Lockdowns were the catechumenate, masks were the religious garb, vaccines were the initiation."

The ruling class was not subtle on this point. New York Governor Kathy Hochul told constituents, "I need you to be my apostles," urging them to spread her gospel on Covid vaccines. Lindsey Graham thanked the divine intervention of mRNA shots. Newspapers ran opinion pieces on why "Jesus would wear a mask." Ibram X. Kendi proudly wrote in *The Atlantic*: "[My] dad likened me to John the Baptist, a voice crying out in the wilderness for racial data on the pandemic." On *The Late Show*, Stephen Colbert parodied The Ten Commandments as a coronavirus warning to worship lockdowns. "Flatten the curve," Colbert's God told the audience. On Easter Sunday 2021, President Biden implored Americans to get the Covid vaccine, insisting it was their "moral obligation," in a speech that did not mention Jesus once.

The Free Expulsion of Religion

Before March 2020, most Americans would think that monitoring church attendance, banning Easter services, and arresting hymn singers were practices reserved for Eastern-style totalitarianism. The Soviet Union persecuted Christians, and the Chinese have Muslim concentration camps, but Americans' freedom of worship is enshrined in the Bill of Rights. The free exercise of religion precedes all other liberties in the First Amendment. Even in the 21st century, when the country had become increasingly secular, few could imagine that political leaders would launch a crusade against organized religion.

Yet, that's exactly what happened. And the assault on religious liberty was not reserved for the piously nonreligious in Santa Barbara or East Hampton. In 2020, Kentucky State Police arrived at an Easter service to issue notices that attendance was criminal. They recorded the congregants' license plate numbers and issued warnings that violators were subject to further sanction.

In Mississippi, police issued citations to a church congregation that hosted a drive-in service despite attendees remaining in their vehicles for the entire service.

In Idaho, police arrested Christians for removing their masks to sing psalms outdoors in September 2020. "We were just singing songs," said Christ Church Pastor Ben Zornes. But that was no excuse for the sin of violating an irrational and unscientific cloth commandment. "At some point in time you have to enforce," the local police chief explained.

The city later reached a settlement that paid $300,000 to Iowans arrested for attending the outdoor service. "[The worshippers] should never have been arrested in the first place, and the constitutionality of what the City thought its Code said is irrelevant," wrote the local district judge. The obviousness of that statement – worshippers should never have been arrested for singing outdoors – reveals the intensity of the secular fervor that swept the country.

Unsurprisingly, Andrew Cuomo was intolerant of citizens worshipping non-political deities.

He threatened upstate New Yorkers with $1,000 fines for attending "drive-in" services in May 2020. "We're not trying to be rebellious," said Pastor Samson Ryman. "We're just trying to be safe and reach our community with the gospel of Jesus Christ in these difficult times when people are having anxiety, worry, different mental concerns, and they want to get some spiritual help, through the word of God." On May 3, 2020, Ryman held his first drive-in service in upstate New York with 23 attendees in 18 vehicles. The next day, Cuomo's police force issued a cease-and-desist letter.

In California, the Santa Clara Health Department used GPS data to monitor congregants at a local evangelical church. The government partnered with a data mining company to create a "geofence" (a digital boundary) around the church's property, monitoring over 65,000 mobile devices to record any citizens that spent more than four minutes in the area.

Around the country, governors deemed churches "non-essential" and barred them from opening their doors. Meanwhile, marijuana dispensaries, liquor stores, abortionists, and lotteries received the protection of the arbitrary label of "essential services." For most of 2020, Christians, Jews, and Muslims had no recourse against the totalitarian assault on their faith and First Amendment freedoms.

Caesars Palace, Calvary Chapel, and the Chief's Cowardice

The orders that shuttered churches were not generally applicable ordinances. They were not blanket decrees that applied equally to all establishments. Instead, states adopted deliberately unequal systems of law: "essential" groups like Costco and casinos could host hundreds of customers at any given time while religious groups faced stringent restrictions or bans. The Supreme Court's Covid docket demonstrated the disparate treatment that targeted churches nationwide.

Before March 2020, the Court's First Amendment jurisprudence was clear: The Free Exercise Clause "protects religious observers against unequal treatment." That includes both "the right to harbor religious beliefs inwardly and secretly" and the "performance of (or abstention from) physical acts." But the Covid creed quickly overturned centuries of legal tradition.

Chief Justice John Roberts put the Free Exercise Clause on hiatus as leaders specifically targeted churches in their decrees. Eventually, a change in the makeup of the Court overturned the unconstitutional attacks on religious liberty.

The Court heard its first case challenging restrictions on religious attendance in May 2020. In *South Bay v. Newsom*, religious groups challenged California Governor Gavin Newsom's executive order that limited church attendance to 25% capacity. They argued that "the fog-of-war" cannot excuse "violating fundamental constitutional rights" and "arbitrarily discriminating against places of worship in violation of their first to the Free Exercise of Religion under the First Amendment."

The Court divided along familiar political lines: the liberal bloc of Justices Ginsburg, Breyer, Sotomayor, and Kagan voted to uphold deprivations of liberty as a valid exercise of states' police power; Justice Gorsuch led conservatives Alito, Kavanaugh, and Thomas in challenging the irrationality of the edicts; Chief Justice Roberts sided with the leftists, abandoning religious freedom by deferring to public health experts.

"Unelected judiciary lacks the background, competence, and expertise to assess public health and is not accountable to the people," the Chief wrote, upholding Newsom's order. And with that, the Chief Justice placed political considerations above the law of the land, deferring to the public health apparatus as constitutional freedoms disappeared from American life. The case had not required him to render a medical opinion; all it required was a basic understanding of the Free Exercise Clause. But worse was yet to come.

In June, the nation erupted in riots in response to the death of George Floyd. Thousands gathered in the streets while cities upheld bans on religious worship. When asked about this double standard, New York City Mayor Bill de Blasio responded, "When you see a nation, an entire nation, simultaneously grappling with an extraordinary crisis seeded in 400 years of American racism, I'm sorry, that is not the same question as the understandably aggrieved store owner or devout religious person who wants to go back to services."

In the *Wall Street Journal*, Abigail Shrier reacted to the double standards imposed on secular and religious gathering with her article "Politicians Shutter Churches and Synagogues, Then Tolerate Riots." She argued:

"Perhaps that 'devout religious person' ought to choose a better hobby, one more meaningful to Mr. de Blasio... California recently issued an order to ease restrictions, setting a 25% occupancy cap on houses of worship but not on retail stores or other businesses—one set of rules for worshipers, another for everyone else. Perhaps most devastating, when petitioners challenged the order at the Supreme Court, the majority shrugged."

The disparate treatment between religious and commercial activities soon became the focus of conservatives on the Supreme Court.

In July, the Court again split 5-4 in its opinion rejecting a Nevada church's challenge to the State's Covid restrictions. Governor Steve Sisolak limited religious gatherings to 50 people. The same order allowed commercial groups, including casinos, to host up to 500 customers. Again, Chief Justice Roberts provided the critical fifth vote in favor of upholding the restriction. Perhaps tellingly, no justice in the majority offered an opinion justifying their rationale.

Citizens quickly recognized how Sisolak's order favored the state's gaming industry over religious services. One local columnist asked, "if a Nevada church were to hold a bingo night in its 500-seat auditorium, under Gov. Steve Sisolak's diktat, 250 people could attend?"

Chief Justice Roberts and the liberal bloc did not offer any explanation for how the 50-person limit could be justified when thousands of protestors gathered the week before, rioting, throwing rocks at officers, and shooting a federal marshal in the head to oppose *systemic racism*. Politically favored groups like Black Lives Matter had no restrictions while church doors remained subject to the capricious whims of "public health" initiatives.

Justice Gorsuch issued a one paragraph dissent criticizing the irrationality of the orders. "Under the Governor's edict, a 10-screen 'multiplex' may host 500 moviegoers at any time. A casino, too, may cater to hundreds at once, with perhaps six people huddled at each craps table here and a similar number gathered around every roulette wheel there," he wrote. But the Governor's order imposed a 50-worshiper limit for religious gatherings, no matter the buildings' capacities. "The First Amendment prohibits such obvious discrimination against the exercise of religion," Gorsuch wrote. "There is no world in which the Constitution permits Nevada to favor Caesars Palace over Calvary Chapel."

Justice Kavanaugh issued a similar dissent, writing: "A State may not impose strict limits on places of worship and looser limits on restaurants, bars, casinos, and gyms, at least without sufficient justification for the differential treatment of religion." The state's largest paper – the *Las Vegas Review-Journal* – noted the majority's failure to explain its decision. "The silence from the majority is significant. These issues aren't going away, and the court will sooner or later have to confront them."

Though Gorsuch had the law and logic on his side, Chief Justice Roberts's deference to the public health apparatus continued the Supreme Court's abandonment of religious liberty. As the *Review-Journal* predicted, the issue continued through the year. Following Justice Ginsburg's death in September 2020, however, the liberal wing could no longer silently uphold tyranny.

In October, Amy Coney Barrett joined the Court and reversed the justices' 5-4 split. One month later, the Court overturned Governor Cuomo's executive order that limited attendance at religious services to 10 people.

Now in the majority, Gorsuch liberated congregants from the tyranny of Cuomo's edicts. He again compared restrictions on secular activities and religious gatherings; "according to the Governor, it may be unsafe to go to church, but it is always fine to pick up another bottle of wine, shop for a new bike, or spend the afternoon exploring your distal points and meridians...Who knew public health would so perfectly align with secular convenience?"

Chief Justice Roberts voted in dissent, though he offered no opinion to justify his view.

In February 2021, California religious organizations again challenged Governor Newsom's Covid restrictions. Newsom had outlawed indoor worship in certain areas and banned singing. Chief Justice Roberts, joined by Kavanaugh and Barrett, upheld the ban on singing but overturned the capacity limits.

Gorsuch wrote a separate opinion, joined by Thomas and Alito, that continued his critiques as Covid entered its second year. He wrote, "Government actors have been moving the goalposts on pandemic-related sacrifices for months, adopting new benchmarks that always seem to put restoration of liberty just around the corner."

Like his opinions in New York and Nevada, he focused on disparate treatment and political favoritism; "if Hollywood may host a studio audience or film a singing competition while not a single soul may enter California's churches, synagogues, and mosques, something has gone seriously awry."

In May 2023, Justice Gorsuch wrote that the responses to

Covid may have been "the greatest intrusions on civil liberties in the peacetime history of this country." The laptop class of the *New York Times* editorial pages responded with scorn, calling Gorsuch's opinion "a shocking worldview but not, in the end, a surprising one."

Notably, the *Times* writers made no effort to deny the Covid responses' vast intrusions on civil liberties. Instead, they argued that American history was based in repression and subjugation, so Gorsuch had no basis for chastising the medical police state of 2020. "Gorsuch's denunciation of pandemic restrictions acts as an inadvertent glimpse into his view of the United States," wrote opinion columnist Jamelle Bouie. "He is willing to ignore or doesn't even see our long, peacetime history of repression and internal tyranny."

Other people have been bad too does not make for an effective legal argument, but no logic or facts could defend the Covid regime. States shuttered churches while offering politically favored groups special privileges. Congregants lost their right to worship and their access to spiritual outlets in times of despair and uncertainty. Across the country, police arrested Americans for attending funerals. Loneliness, suicide, and substance abuse skyrocketed. Citizens remained free to stand next to their neighbors at the liquor store or the blackjack table, so long as they didn't attend worship beforehand. The elderly were left without comfort in their final days. Catholics missed their last rites; at other times, they were forced to hear them through an iPhone speaker. Governors and mayors banned the celebration of holidays. They criminalized the communal nature of religious gatherings.

"An American mayor criminalized the communal celebration of Easter," wrote U.S. District Justin Walker after Louisville's prohibition of holiday drive-in services. "That sentence is one that this court never expected to see outside the pages of a dystopian novel, or perhaps the pages of The Onion." Yet that dystopia became reality across the country. Religious groups became the target of authoritarian crusades.

"Plague on a Biblical Scale"

New York City Bill de Blasio was particularly proud of his stand against religious freedom during the pandemic. In April 2020, a Jewish community in Brooklyn held a funeral for a local rabbi. Masked mourners walked with the coffin through the streets. Their leaders announced social distancing precautions, but their efforts were insufficient for their self-annointed dictator.

The six-foot, five-inch de Blasio led hundreds of police officers into Brooklyn to take on crowds of unarmed Orthodox Jews. "Something absolutely unacceptable happened in Williamsburg tonite: a large funeral gathering in the middle of this pandemic," the mayor posted. "When I heard, I went there myself to ensure the crowd was dispersed. And what I saw WILL NOT be tolerated so long as we are fighting the Coronavirus."

De Blasio and hundreds of masked policemen stopped the funeral, setting up a battle between religious liberty and the mayor's unscientific edicts. "My message to the Jewish community, and all communities, is this simple: the time for warnings has passed," de Blasio later posted. "This is about stopping this disease and saving lives. Period."

The media encouraged the mayor's crusade. The *New York Times* warned that Covid threatened a "Plague on a Biblical Scale" to Hasidic communities. Notably, de Blasio and the *Times* did not issue similar warnings when thousands of BLM supporters stormed through New York, looting stores, destroying police cars, and assaulting officers.

As the *New York Times* explained on June 2, 2020:

"The looters tore off the plywood that boarded up Macy's flagship store in Herald Square, swarming by the dozens inside to steal whatever they could find before being chased down by the police. Others smashed the windows at a Nike store, grabbing shirts, jeans and zip-up jackets. They crashed into a Coach store, ransacked a Bergdorf Goodman branch and destroyed scores of smaller storefronts along the way."

But the "time for warnings" had not passed for Black Lives Matter. De Blasio did not personally escort his police force to the scene to quash the urban anarchy. He did not describe the vandalism, crime, and demonic mobs as "absolutely unacceptable." That treatment was reserved for peaceful religious gatherings. As the mayor explained, activists using *racism* as an excuse to unravel society was "not the same question" as a "devout religious person" attending service.

Instead, de Blasio deliberately held back policemen during the riots to avoid potential backlash from his left-wing supporters. "As a result, knowing they were outnumbered, officers were unwilling to take on the looters," claimed Governor Cuomo's top aide, Melissa DeRosa.

After Chief Justice Roberts suspended the First Amendment in May 2020, the assault on religious liberty continued through the summer. Governor Cuomo specifically targeted Jewish gatherings in an October 2020 press conference. "Orthodox Jewish gatherings often are very, very large, and we've seen what one person can do in a group," he complained. He chastised them for hosting outdoor meetings that violated his social distancing directives.

Brooklyn Jews protested in response, though they refrained

from looting local Nike and Macy's stores for sneakers and designer jeans. "We are not going to be deprived of the right that we have in America, like everybody else in America, the right to observe our religion," City Councilman Kalman Yeger told a crowd.

Weeks later, Justice Barrett joined the Court and restored that right to New Yorkers. Despite the Jewish community's ongoing Covid transgressions, the *plague of a Biblical scale* never arrived. As of 2025, de Blasio and Cuomo remain unrepentant.

The restrictions were not just bad public policy; they overturned the First Amendment's Free Exercise Clause. Governors and police forces criminalized worship and targeted religious gatherings. They used the threat of force and the country's largest police department to crack down on worship.

A secular fervor overtook the country in 2020. The rule of law gave way to the panic of fear. Governors and mayors embraced their new power to control their citizens. The Chief Justice invented a pandemic exception to the First Amendment, enabling the assaults on worship as Americans lost their most precious liberties. The lockdowns featured deliberate and targeted attacks on religious freedoms while offering brazenly irrational exceptions to political allies and commercial enterprises. Shuttering churches had no relation to viral spread of the disease; it was a loyalty test designed to replace worship of the eternal with devotion to the political.

VOTING

In 1845, Congress established Election Day as the Tuesday after the first Monday of November in order "to establish a uniform time" for Americans to cast their ballots for president. Historically, voters needed to provide a valid reason – such as illness or military service – to qualify for absentee ballots.

But Covid served as a pretext to overturn that tradition. As the political actors used the guise of "public health" to amass political power in March 2020, the looming presidential election was the zenith of their aspirations. Just 25% of votes in 2020 occurred at the polls on Election Day. Mail-in voting more than doubled. Key swing states eliminated the need to provide a valid reason to cast absentee ballots. The virus and *racial justice* became justifications to disregard verification methods like signature requirements.

Rejection rates for absentee ballots plummeted by more than 80% in some states as the Covid regime welcomed an unprecedented increase in mail-in voting. Politicians and media outlets ignored rampant voter fraud in the months leading up to the election. They treated concerns surrounding absentee voting as obscure conspiracy theories despite a bipartisan commission describing it as "the largest source of potential voter fraud" just a decade earlier.

It is now clear that the overhaul of our election system was a deliberate initiative from the outset of the pandemic response. In March 2020, when the Government's official policy was still "Two weeks to flatten the curve," the administrative state began instituting the infrastructure to hijack the November presidential election, more than 30 weeks beyond when the Covid response was supposed to end.

March 2020: The CDC and the CARES Act Meddle in the Election

On March 12, 2020, the CDC issued a recommendation for states and localities to "encourage voters to use voting methods that minimize direct contact with other people," including "mail-in methods of voting." Two weeks later, President Trump signed the $2 trillion CARES Act, which offered states $400 million to re-engineer their election processes for that November.

At the time, proponents of the CARES Act argued it was necessary to reopen the country. The *New York Times* editorialized that it was "critical to fund and implement the safety measures necessary to let Americans get back to work, school and play without a recurrence of the virus." But political actors immediately plotted ways to use the funds to entrench their power long past the proposed two-week lockdowns. Nearly every swing state announced plans to promote mail-in voting and reduce electoral safeguards in a Congressional report.

"Michigan will use the funds to bolster vote by mail," the report announced. Governor Gretchen Whitmer received $11.3 million from the CARES Act to change election procedures in her state. In November, 57% of Michigan voters (over 3 million people) cast their ballot by mail. For the first time, the state did not require a reason for absentee voting, and mail-in ballots more than doubled. President Trump would go on to lose Michigan by just 150,000 votes.

When Trump signed the CARES Act, just 0.05% of Michigan residents had tested positive for Covid. The state's political leaders later boasted that their agenda had not been focused on public health. "Even when there's not a pandemic, once people begin using the absentee ballot process, they're much more likely to continue to do so in the future," said Michigan Secretary of State Jocelyn Benson after Election Day.

Pennsylvania received $14.2 million from the CARES Act to address its election process. At the time, the infection rate in the Keystone State was 1 in 6,000 (0.017%). Democratic Governor Tom Wolf's administration told the federal government it would use its plans to increase absentee voting. In November, 2.5 million Pennsylvanians voted by mail. President Biden won 75% of those votes – a difference of 1.4 million. President Trump lost the state by under 100,000 votes.

The CARES Act provided Wisconsin with over $7 million for election matters. Democratic Governor Tom Evers said the state would use funds to provide "absentee ballot envelopes," to develop "the statewide voter registration system and online absentee ballot request portal," and "to account for additional costs" related to mail-in voting.

Governor Evers explained, "Having as many absentee ballots as possible is absolutely a top priority [and] always has been given the emergency we're in." Eight months later, 1.9 million of the state's 3.3 million voters cast their ballot by mail. The rejection rate for absentee ballots plummeted from 1.4% in 2016 to 0.2%. President Biden won Wisconsin by just 20,000 votes.

Democratic activists were unsatisfied with the $400 million added to the national debt to reshape the elections. Mark Zuckerberg's foundation provided absentee activists with an additional $300 million. In *Time*, Molly Ball celebrated the "shadow campaign that saved the 2020 election." She quoted Amber McReynolds, the president of "nonpartisan National Vote at Home Institute," who called the government's reluctance to provide *additional* funding "a failure at the federal level." Despite her professed "non-partisanship," President Biden rewarded her service by appointing her to the Board of the US Postal Service.

In *Time*, Ball hailed the mail-in activists' efforts, which included targeting "Black voters" who may have otherwise "preferred to exercise their franchise in person." They focused on social media outreach to try to convince people that a "prolonged [vote] count wasn't a sign of problems." Their informational warfare may have changed Americans' perception on mail-in voting, but it could not eradicate the predictable controversies that it created.

Spring 2020: Voter Fraud Skyrockets

In May 2020, New Jersey held municipal elections and required all voting take place via mail. The State's third largest city, Paterson, held its election for City Council. The results should have been a national scandal that ended the push for mail-in voting.

Shortly after the election, the Postal Service discovered "hundreds of mail-in ballots" in one town mailbox. A Snapchat video showed a man named Abu Razyen illegally handling a stack of ballots he said was for candidate Shanin Khalique. Khalique initially defeated his opponent by just eight votes. A recount found their vote was tied.

Paterson resident Ramona Javier never received her mail-in ballot for the election. Neither did eight of her family members and neighbors, yet they were all listed as having voted. "We did not receive vote-by-mail ballots and thus we did not vote," she told the press. "This is corruption. This is fraud."

Election officials rejected 19% of the ballots from Paterson, a city with over 150,000 residents. While Paterson's election was particularly troublesome, mail-in ballots were problematic across the state. Thirty other New Jersey municipalities held vote-by-mail elections that day, and the average disqualification rate was 9.6%.

New Jersey brought voting fraud charges against City Councilman Michael Jackson, Councilman-Elect Alex Mendez, and two other men for their "criminal conduct involving mail-in ballots during the election." All four were charged with illegally collecting, procuring, and submitting mail-in ballots. A state judge later ordered a new vote, finding that the May election "was not the fair, free and full expression of the intent of the voters. It was rife with mail in vote procedural violations constituting nonfeasance and malfeasance."

Politicians refused to concede that the incident revealed the vulnerability of absentee balloting. Instead, Governor Phil Murphy told the press that the scandal was a good sign. "I view that as a positive data point," he argued. "Some guys tried to screw around with the system. They got caught by law enforcement. They've been indicted. They'll pay a price." Murphy and other allies of Joe Biden ignored the threat, presuming the forces would not hurt their hopes that November.

In Wisconsin, the April 2020 primary election offered further evidence of the challenges and corruption surrounding mail-in voting. Following the primary, a postal center outside Milwaukee discovered three tubs of absentee ballots that never reached their intended recipients. Fox Point, a village outside Milwaukee, has a population of under 7,000 people.

Beginning in March, Fox Point received between 20 and 50 undelivered absentee ballots per day. In the weeks leading up to the election, the village manager said that increased to between 100 and 150 ballots per day. On election day, the town received a plastic mail bin with 175 unmailed ballots. "We're not sure why this happened," said the village manager. "Nobody seems to be able to tell me why."

Democrats admitted the system threatened election integrity. "This has all the makings of a Florida 2000 if we have a close race," said Gordon Hintz, the Democratic minority leader in the Wisconsin State Assembly. New York Governor Andrew Cuomo went further. "It's a harder system to administer, and obviously it's a harder system to police writ large," he said. Cuomo continued, "People showing up, people actually showing ID, is still the easiest system to assure total integrity."

The Wisconsin primary also featured special elections for the Wisconsin Supreme Court. A liberal judge upset the incumbent conservative justice, and partisans embraced their overhaul of the electoral system. The *New York Times* reported: "Wisconsin Democrats are working to export their template for success – intense digital outreach and a well-coordinated vote-by-mail operation – to other states in the hope that it will improve the party's chances in local and statewide elections and in the quest to unseat President Trump in November."

Despite the corruption, the lost ballots, and the admissions of threats to electoral integrity, the process had been a success in political terms; their candidate had won. The ends had justified the means. Citizens lost faith in their election process, and political leaders readily admitted that their concerns were justified; but the professional politicos and their mouthpiece, the *New York Times*, characterized the disaster as a "template for success."

Controversies continued to emerge surrounding mail-in ballots. In September 2020, a government contractor threw Trump mail-in ballots in the trash in Pennsylvania. ABC News reported that "ballots had been found in a dumpster next to the elections building." A week later, trays of absentee ballots were found in a ditch in Wisconsin. In Nevada, the Reno-Sparks Indian Colony offered gifts, including gift cards, jewelry, and clothing to Native Americans who showed up to vote. Activist Bethany Sam organized the event, where she donned a Biden-Harris mask and stood in front of the Biden-Harris campaign bus.

Voters in California received ballots with no place to vote for president, over 20% of ballots mailed to voters in Teaneck, New Jersey, had the wrong Congressional districts listed, and Franklin County, Ohio reported sending over 100,000 absentee ballots to the wrong address due to an "envelope stuffing error."

In October, Texas police arrested Carrollton Mayoral Candidate Zul Mirza Mohamed on 109 counts of fraud for forging mail-in ballots. Authorities discovered fraudulent ballots at Mohamed's residence with fictitious licenses. That same month, a Pennsylvania district attorney charged Lehigh County Elections Judge Everett "Erika" Bickford with "prying into ballots" and altering the entries from a local election that June. That election was decided by just 55 votes.

Reports continued to emerge after the election. The *New York Post* uncovered election records that showed dead people had cast absentee ballots that November. California law enforcement charged two men with a 41-count criminal complaint for allegedly submitting over 8,000 fraudulent voter registration applications on behalf of homeless people. Their goal was to get Carlos Montenegro, one of the defendants, elected Mayor of Hawthorne, a city in Los Angeles County. The state also alleged that Montenegro committed perjury by falsifying names and signatures in his paperwork for his mayoral campaign.

In 2022, a Georgia investigation found more than 1,000 absentee ballots that never left the Cobb County government facility. Two months earlier, mail-in ballots from the 2020 election were discovered in a Baltimore USPS facility. In 2023, Michigan police found hundreds of mail-in ballots from the 2020 election in a township clerk's storage unit.

All of this was entirely predictable, but perhaps that was the point. From the outset, the Covid regime sought to abolish the safeguards of our election system despite well-known concerns regarding election integrity.

The United States of Amnesia: Voter Fraud Was Nothing New

*Absentee ballots remain the largest
source of potential voter fraud.*

The Covid regime's messaging was clear: only conspiratorial lunatics would question the integrity of an election system that more than doubles its mail-in voting. FBI Director Christopher Wray testified, "We have not seen, historically, any kind of coordinated national voter fraud effort in a major election, whether it's by mail or otherwise."

But this wasn't true. Wray's lie contradicted longstanding conclusions regarding electoral integrity. Just as the public health apparatus abandoned thousands of years of epidemiological practice to implement lockdowns, the media and elected officials abandoned principles that until that moment had been common sense.

Following the controversy of the 2000 Bush-Gore Presidential election, the United States formed a bipartisan Commission on

Federal Election Reform. President Jimmy Carter, a Democrat, and former Secretary of State James Baker, a Republican, chaired the group.

After five years of research, the group published its final report – "Building Confidence in U.S. Elections." It offered a series of recommendations to reduce voter fraud, including enacting voter-ID laws and limiting absentee voting. The commission was unequivocal: "Absentee ballots remain the largest source of potential voter fraud."

The report continued: "Citizens who vote at home, at nursing homes, at the workplace, or in church are more susceptible to pressure, overt and subtle, or to intimidation. Vote buying schemes are far more difficult to detect when citizens vote by mail."

The findings were reinforced by subsequent election scandals. A 2012 *New York Times* headline read: "Error and Fraud at Issue as Absentee Voting Rises." The article made the front page of the paper and echoed the concerns of the Carter-Baker Commission. "Fraud Easier via Mail," the paper explained.

"You could steal some absentee ballots or stuff a ballot box or bribe an election administrator or fiddle with an electronic voting machine," said Yale Law professor Heather Gerken. That explains, she said, "why all the evidence of stolen elections involves absentee ballots and the like."

The *Times* continued the potential corruption of mail-in ballots. "On the most basic level, absentee voting replaces the oversight that exists at polling places with something akin to an honor system," the author wrote. The *Times* then cited US Circuit Court Judge Richard A. Posner: "Absentee voting is to voting in person as a take-home exam is to a proctored one."

The report went on: "Voters in nursing homes can be subjected to subtle pressure, outright intimidation or fraud. The secrecy of their voting is easily compromised. And their ballots can be intercepted both coming and going."

Historic controversies supported this consensus. The 1997 Miami mayoral election resulted in 36 arrests for absentee-ballot fraud. A judge voided the results and ordered the city to hold a new election due to "a pattern of fraudulent, intentional, and criminal conduct." The results were reversed in the subsequent election.

Following Dallas's 2017 City Council race, authorities sequestered 700 mail-in ballots signed "Jose Rodriguez." Elderly voters alleged that party activists had forged their signatures on their mail-in ballots. Miguel Hernandez later pled guilty to the crime of forging their signatures after collecting unfilled ballots, and using them to support his candidate of choice.

In 2018, the Democratic National Commission challenged an Arizona law that set safeguards around absentee voting, including limiting who could handle mail-in ballots. US District Judge Douglas L. Rayes, an Obama appointee, upheld the law. "Indeed, mail-in ballots by their very nature are less secure than ballots cast in person at polling locations," he wrote. He found that "the prevention of voter fraud and preservation of public confidence in election integrity" were important state interests and cited the Carter-Baker Commission's finding that "absentee ballots remain the largest source of potential voter fraud."

The rest of the world recognizes the obvious threat that mail-in voting poses to election integrity. In 1975, France banned postal ballots after rampant voter fraud. Ballots were cast with the names of dead Frenchmen, and political activists in Corsica stole ballots and bribed voters. In 1991, Mexico mandated voter photo IDs and banned absentee ballots after the Institutional Revolutionary Party repeatedly committed fraud to maintain power. In Austria, Belgium, Canada, Chile, Denmark, Estonia, Ireland, Lithuania,

Luxembourg, Poland, Portugal, Slovenia, Spain, Turkey, and the United Kingdom, photo ID is required to get an absentee ballot.

In August 2020, economist John Lott analyzed how Covid was being used as a pretext to overhaul electoral standards in the United States. He wrote:

"Thirty-seven states have so far changed their mail-in voting procedures this year in response to the Coronavirus. Despite frequent claims that President Trump's warning about vote fraud/voting buying with mail-in ballots is "baselessly" or "without evidence" about mail-in vote fraud, there are numerous examples of vote fraud and vote buying with mail-in ballots in the United States and across the world. Indeed, concerns over vote fraud and vote buying with mail-in ballots causes (sic) the vast majority of countries to ban mail-in voting unless the citizen is living abroad.

There are fraud problems with mail-in absentee ballots but the problems with universal mail-in ballots are much more significant. Still most countries ban even absentee ballots for people living in their countries.

Most developed countries ban absentee ballots unless the citizen is living abroad or require Photo-IDs to obtain those ballots. Even higher percentages of European Union or other European countries ban absentee for in country voters."

Political actors treated opposition to absentee balloting with scorn while ignoring its history of corruption. Mail-in voting may have been the decisive factor in the 2020 election, but Trump and his allies searched for other explanations to avoid his complicity in signing the CARES Act.

The Trump campaign promised to produce "irrefutable"

evidence that proved Trump won the election "in a landslide." "I'm going to release the Kraken," one Trump election lawyer told Lou Dobbs in November 2020. President Trump and Rudy Giuliani tweeted blame at Dominion voting machines. Sean Hannity said privately that Giuliani was "acting like an insane person."

Two days later, Hannity told viewers about a "software error" from Dominion that "wrongfully awarded Joe Biden thousands of ballots that were cast for President Trump, until the problem was amazingly fixed." In August 2023, Trump announced that he would release an "irrefutable report" demonstrating voter fraud in Georgia. He canceled the announcement two days later.

In the process, they ignored a far more obvious explanation. The first six Presidential elections of the 21st century were decided by an average of 44 electoral votes. Pennsylvania, Georgia, Michigan, and Wisconsin offer a combined 62 votes in the Electoral College.

Following the 2020 overhaul of our election system, California, New York, Pennsylvania, and Nevada allowed voting in person without any form of identification. Michigan allowed voting without photo identification. Under the pretext of Covid and racial justice, states abolished their electoral safeguards. They turned Election Day into a month of voting. After prominent Democrats refused to certify the 2000, 2004, and 2016 elections, the victors chastised any concerns for electoral integrity as attacks on democracy.

In *Tablet Magazine*, Armin Rosen explained that two forces catalyzed the "stealth revolution" that activists launched to abolish electoral safeguards under the pretext of Covid.

"The first was the Democratic Party's decision to treat Donald Trump not as a despicable outcome of the country's normal democratic process but as a dictator-in-waiting who had stolen the presidency with help from the Kremlin and now wanted to end democracy... This emergency was in turn used to justify any number of extrademocratic theories and measures—from the promulgation of hallucinatory conspiracies with the help of law enforcement and the intelligence community, to overt attempts to control and censor the news—on the grounds that such excesses were needed to save democracy from itself."

Second, Covid "created a situation in which 'exceptions' to existing laws seemed normal and natural enough that a large part of the population welcomed them, or at least treated them as the one-time cost of holding a national election during a plague year... The incumbent party was caught off guard by a well-organized and well-funded effort among Democratic lawyers and NGOs to overhaul voting procedures in key states."

Rosen concluded: "The changes to voting laws that happened across the country in 2020 were not simply fear-driven or well-meaning responses to a global pandemic. Rather, COVID and the resulting panic became an opportunity for partisan activists and lawyers to rapidly accelerate changes to American voting practices that were already high up on their agendas."

But Democratic operatives were not content with their victory in 2020; they launched an operation to censor, smear, and destroy any actors who pushed back against their newly adopted political strategy. No political actor has been more influential in that effort than Marc Elias. Elias, the nation's most prominent election attorney, led the crusade to overturn the Wisconsin Supreme Court's 2022 ruling in *Teigen v. Wisconsin Elections Commission*, which banned the use of "drop boxes" in the state.

In deciding whether to hear the case, Republican Justice

Rebecca Bradley called the Elias-led litigation a "shameless effort to readjust the balance of political power in Wisconsin." Elias was successful, and Wisconsin was required to adopt dropboxes despite the state's concerns. Similarly, Elias led lawsuits to defend dropboxes in Pennsylvania leading up to the 2024 election.

Elias then worked to personally destroy the careers of his opponents. Along with Project 65, a nonprofit affiliated with the Democrat Party, Elias has called for the disbarment of attorneys who challenge him in court. "I don't think any lawyer should have a bar license for the privilege of destroying our country's democratic traditions," Elias insists, though "democratic traditions" apparently mean months of absentee voting without signature verification or photo identification. He demanded an "accountability structure" for those who challenge the Democrats' mandated standards for a "free and fair election," in a call for Soviet-style reforms where elections are *free* provided you don't criticize the incumbent.

The liberalization of voting laws was integral to the pandemic response. This process was justified based on nonscientific grounds while invoking the cover of science. Then, the regime dedicated itself to destroying anyone who opposed their election manipulation. The disease did not cause the dramatic upheaval of the American system of voting; it was the fear of the result that shocked the country four years earlier.

NO PLACE TO HIDE

By April 2020, Americans were living in a regime of government surveillance that would have been previously unrecognizable. Politicians, newspapers, and activists touted a "Manhattan Project-level operation" aimed at enforcing lockdown orders via mass surveillance and house arrest orders. While insisting their operations were in support of public health, they used familiar tracking programs that obliterated the safeguards of our Fourth Amendment. Silicon Valley forged lucrative partnerships with state and national governments, selling users' habits and movements without their consent. Rather suddenly, supposedly free citizens were the subject of "track and trace" programs as if they were UPS packages.

"You never want a serious crisis to go to waste," Rahm Emanuel famously remarked. "And what I mean by that is an opportunity to do things that you think you could not do before." State actors and tech profiteers embraced Emanuel's philosophy in the Covid response. They took advantage of the nation's fear to implement programs that abolished the Fourth Amendment. Technology companies saw massive gains as they implemented a panopticon that allowed law enforcement to track any citizen in any place at any time. Coronamania was an *opportunity to do things that they couldn't do before*, and the results were lucrative. The wealth of billionaires increased more in the first two years of the pandemic than it had in the previous 23 years combined, primarily due to gains in the tech sector.

In 1975, Senator Frank Church led a government investigation into US intelligence agencies. Speaking of their covert power 50 years ago, Church warned, "That capability at any time could be turned around on the American people, and no American would have any privacy left, such is the capability to monitor everything: telephone conversations, telegrams, it doesn't matter. There would be no place to hide."

Not only did the government turn its surveillance powers on the citizenry, but it recruited the most powerful information companies in world history to advance its agenda, leaving Americans poorer, less free, and with no place to hide. Big Tech and government agencies colluded to abolish the Fourth Amendment safeguards that previously protected Americans against surveillance. This process siphoned tax dollars to the country's wealthiest industry, forcing citizens to subsidize the evisceration of their liberties.

A Safeguard Against Tyranny

The Fourth Amendment guarantees the right to be free from unreasonable government searches and seizures. The Supreme Court has repeatedly ruled that the state cannot utilize new technologies to circumvent its protections. In 2018, the Court held in *Carpenter v. United States* that the Government violated the Fourth Amendment when it obtained a citizen's cell phone location data from his wireless carrier. Chief Justice Roberts wrote that the Fourth Amendment's "basic purpose" is to "safeguard the privacy and security of individuals against arbitrary invasions by government officials." Government "could not capitalize" on the technology to evade constitutional scrutiny.

The *Carpenter* Court cited Americans' right to protect their record of "physical movements" from Government surveillance. "Mapping a cell phone's location, " the Court explained, creates an "all-encompassing" and unconstitutional "record of the holder's whereabouts."

Before March 2020, the law was clear: Silicon Valley's latest fads did not create a government loophole for impermissible searches. Suddenly, the panic surrounding the coronavirus obliterated the safeguards of the Fourth Amendment, and Americans sacrificed their privacy to private-public partnerships. State and federal agencies used mobile data to track and trace American citizens, utilizing new technologies to infringe upon their rights. This surveillance state became supra-national as Silicon Valley giants partnered with countries across the world to expand the tyranny beyond geographic borders.

From Snowden to Covid

The foundations of the Covid panopticon – public-private collusion, mass surveillance, and domestic spying – started long before 2020. In 2013, a 29-year-old NSA contractor discovered illegal mass surveillance programs while working on a Hawaii base. He raised his concerns to the appropriate internal channels, but supervisors repeatedly ignored his reports. He boarded a flight to Hong Kong with thousands of classified NSA documents and met with a group of journalists, including Glenn Greenwald.

The reports revealed that the National Security Agency (NSA) had conducted a secret program of mass government surveillance that logged millions of Americans' phone calls and communications. They directly contradicted the sworn testimony of Director of National Intelligence James Clapper from just months before. "Does the NSA collect any type of data at all on millions or hundreds of millions of Americans?" asked Senator Ron Wyden. Clapper responded, "No, sir... not wittingly."

The documents uncovered by Edward Snowden exposed a litany of crimes, including Clapper's brazen perjury. The Intelligence Community had logged the phone calls, emails, and financial information of millions of Americans. In a preview of 2020, the Snowden reports revealed the tyrannical merger of state and corporate power. AT&T and Western Union sold bulk records of phone calls and international money transfers to the CIA. The NSA collected telephone records from Verizon that detailed millions of Americans' call logs on an "ongoing, daily basis" through a secret court order.

Snowden also revealed a covert government operation called "Prism" that gave the NSA direct access to citizens' data from tech companies including Facebook, Google, and Apple. Without any public debate, the Intelligence Community had access to citizens' search history, file transfers, live chats, and email communications.

Two U.S. Courts of Appeal later ruled that the NSA's warrantless spying program was illegal. In *ACLU v. Clapper*, the Second Circuit wrote that the "bulk collection of data as to essentially the entire population of the United States...permits the development of a government database with a potential for invasions of privacy unimaginable in the past." The Ninth Circuit later cited Snowden's revelations half a dozen times in its unanimous opinion ruling that the bulk collection of Americans' metadata is illegal.

Congress codified these holdings into law, and President Obama signed the USA Freedom Act into law in 2015, outlawing the bulk collection of Americans' metadata. The law did little to curb the

Intelligence Community's extra-constitutional pursuits. In 2021, US Senators revealed that the CIA continued its domestic spying operations. "...Congress's clear intent, expressed over many years and through multiple pieces of legislation, to limit, and in some cases, prohibit the warrantless collection of Americans' records," wrote Senators Ron Wyden and Martin Heinrich to the CIA Director and Director of National Intelligence. "Yet, throughout this period, the CIA has secretly conducted its own bulk program." Other agencies were guilty as well. The FBI and the Department of Homeland Security admitted to purchasing precise GPS data from mobile phone companies.

The Intelligence Community's disdain for Americans' privacy and disregard for constitutional liberties set the stage for the Covid crisis to usher in a new era of mass surveillance.

March 2020: No Place to Hide

Central governments immediately pushed for digital surveillance as Covid cases rose in March 2020. On March 17, the *Wall Street Journal* reported, "government agencies are putting in place or considering a range of tracking and surveillance technologies that test the limits of personal privacy." The White House launched a task force with tech companies including Google, Facebook, and Amazon. The CDC partnered with Palantir to launch data collection and contact tracing initiatives. The EU requested that European telecommunications companies share users' mobile data "for the common good" amid the spread of Covid-19.

The WHO called on nations to track smartphones to monitor and enforce isolation orders. "It is all very well and good to say self-isolate, now is the time to say it must be done," said Marylouise McLaws, an advisor to the WHO's Infection Prevention and Control Global Unit. As McLaws indicated, technological surveillance was a means for demanding compliance and ensuring that *it must be done*. A police force could not contain millions of citizens, but digital platforms enabled mass surveillance, and, in turn, mass compliance.

In the UK, Prime Minister Boris Johnson invited more than 30 technology companies to join the government in its efforts against Covid. British scientists called on the companies (which included Google, Apple, Facebook, and Amazon) to "invest in society" by turning over customers' data to the government. They wrote in the scientific journal *Nature*:

> "Digital data from billions of mobile phones and footprints from web searches and social media remain largely inaccessible to researchers and governments. These data could support community surveillance, contact tracing, social mobilisation, health promotion, communication with the public and evaluation of public health interventions."

Unlike the Snowden controversy, the proponents of state authority were straightforward with their aims. The program was designed to implement *community surveillance*. Within weeks, Amazon, Microsoft, and Palantir agreed to contracts to share citizens' data with the British government. In the US, state agencies met with Silicon Valley companies to develop facial recognition systems and data-mining technology to track infected citizens. The Federal Government used data from Google and Facebook to track citizens' GPS locations.

By May, nearly 30 countries were using data from cell phone companies to track citizens. "This is a Manhattan Project-level problem that is being addressed by people all over the place," John Scott-Railton, a senior researcher at Citizen Lab, a research center at the University of Toronto, told the *Washington Post.* The article continued:

> "In a matter of months, tens of millions of people in dozens of countries have been placed under surveillance. Governments, private companies and researchers observe the health, habits and movements of citizens, often without their consent. It is a massive effort, aimed at enforcing quarantine rules or tracing the spread of the coronavirus, that has sprung up pell-mell in country after country."

Just two months earlier, that article would have been unrecognizable for Americans. *Tens of millions of people placed under surveillance, often without their consent in a Manhattan Project-level operation aimed at enforcing quarantine (house arrest) rules.* That type of dystopian hellscape sounded extreme even for authoritarians in China, yet the United States embraced the program within six weeks of Covid reaching its shores.

In April 2020, the *New York Times* touted a contact tracing program "that would previously be considered unimaginable." The article's blueprint came from the Center for American Progress, a liberal think tank founded by Democratic operative John Podesta and funded by Bill Gates, George Soros, and the Pharmaceutical Research and Manufacturers of America (Big Pharma's lobbying entity). The *Times* marketed the proposal for an "enormous information technology monitoring system" that would use Americans' cell phone data "to monitor where they go and whom they get near, which would allow contact tracing to be done instantaneously."

The United States adopted the core proposals of the Center for American Progress. Later that month, the Department of Health and Human Services agreed to two multi-million contracts with

Palantir to monitor citizens in response to Covid. Five months later, the National Institute of Health awarded Palantir a government contract to build the "largest centralized collection of Covid-19 data in the world." State governments used cell phone data to track citizens and punish the non-compliant. As Senator Church warned, there was "no place to hide," and the powerful enjoyed massive windfalls.

"The new normal" was immensely profitable for tech companies that partnered with government agencies. Palantir went public in September 2020. Three months later, its market cap had skyrocketed to ten times its IPO value. From March 2020 to June 2023, Amazon's market cap increased by 40%, Google's increased by 75%, and Apple's increased by 127%.

Covid accelerated a process in which centralized powers weaponized data in the pursuit of social control and profit. The full extent of the surveillance state remains unclear, but independent programs suggest that the Covid response eradicated the privacy that the Fourth Amendment was designed to protect. Warrantless tracking targeted the enemies of the Covid state, including churchgoers, the unvaccinated, and the working class. More alarmingly, global power structures are eager to repurpose Covid tracing programs to implement a permanent system of mass surveillance.

Tracking Church Attendance

In May 2022, Vice revealed that the CDC purchased cell phone data from Silicon Valley company SafeGraph to track the location of tens of millions of Americans during Covid. At first, the agency used this data to track compliance with lockdown orders, vaccine promotions, and other Covid-related initiatives. The agency explained that the "mobility data" would be available for further "agency-wide use" and "numerous CDC priorities," including monitoring religious observation.

SafeGraph sold this information to federal bureaucrats, who then used the data to spy on millions of Americans' behavior. The tracking included information on where they visited and whether they complied with house arrest orders. Unshackled from Constitutional restraints, bureaucrats tracked Americans' movements, religious observances, and medical activity.

In California, the Santa Clara County Health Department purchased cellular mobility data from SafeGraph to target religious observance. The company collected GPS locations and aggregated data on 65,000 users' locations. They used this information - known as points of interests (POIs) – and sold it to government agencies. In Santa Clara, they focused their attention on a local evangelical church called Calvary Chapel.

SafeGraph and the local government created a digital boundary - known as a "geofence" - around Calvary Chapel's property and monitored cellular devices that spent time within the geographic limits of the church. County officials insist that the GPS data remained anonymous, but journalist David Zweig explains that the anonymity is easily cracked:

"The SafeGraph data ostensibly does not provide personal information on individuals. Yet I spoke with a scientist who utilizes similar data in their work who said it would, of course, be easy to identify an individual user. You can track the location at one POI, in this case the church, and then follow the device back to its home address…an entity could easily figure out individuals' identities if SafeGraph gave them the data."

The "anonymous" data does not prevent groups from identifying the user. In 2020, a Catholic news site deanonymized a Wisconsin priest's data to reveal that he had visited gay bars. In 2021, Google banned SafeGraph from its app store after pro-choice activists warned that the data could be used to track women who visit abortion clinics.

With the aid of digital surveillance, Santa Clara implemented a police state. In August 2020, the county established a "civil enforcement program" to investigate and punish violations of the health department's orders. That month, enforcement officers targeted the church with financial punishment. By October, the county had fined Calvary $350,000.

Their high-tech totalitarianism inadvertently revealed the arbitrary and capricious nature of government lockdowns. As Santa Clara tracked its citizens, it monitored the most popular areas in the county. By Thanksgiving 2020, the six busiest locations in the area were shopping centers and malls. Unlike local churches, the commercial groups did not have bans on indoor gatherings. While the county ordered stakeouts, on-site surveillance, and recordings at Calvary Chapel, the strip malls and shopping centers did not face harassment from law enforcement. The "geofences" proved to be compliance tests, devoid of reason.

The essence of the program would have been considered un-American before the Covid Coup. Nine months before the coronavirus emerged, the *New York Times* decried how the Chinese had created a "virtual cage" through a digital information program that "taps into networks of neighborhood informants" and "tracks individuals and analyzes their behavior." The article described the system of "high-tech surveillance" that President Xi implemented to stifle dissent and restrict liberty. "The goal here is instilling fear – fear that their surveillance technology can see into every corner of your life," Wang Lixiong, a Chinese author, told the *Times*. "The amount of people and equipment used for security is part of the deterrent effect."

One year later, the United States had set up its own system of "virtual cages." Ultimately, the goal was the same: instill fear, demand conformity, deter dissent. By tracking citizens, they could look into every corner of Americans' lives, arbitrarily enforcing punishment against the disfavored.

MassNotify and Mass Surveillance

In Massachusetts, the state Department of Public Health worked with Google to secretly install Covid-tracing software on citizens' smartphones. The state launched "MassNotify" in April 2021, but few citizens downloaded the app. Two months later, the state and Google worked together to secretly install the program on over one million mobile devices without owners' consent or knowledge. If users discovered the program and deleted it, the Department of Public Health reinstalled the program onto their phones, again without their approval.

"MassNotify" used Bluetooth to constantly interact with nearby devices and create an ongoing log of users' locations. That information was time-stamped and stored with the users' personal identifiers, including wireless IP addresses, phone numbers, and personal email accounts. That data was available to the State, Google, network providers, and other third parties. Those groups could then identify the individuals and their corresponding data logs. In sum, the Government gained access to a digital timeline of their movements, contacts, and personal information.

This clearly violated Supreme Court precedent. In 2018, the Supreme Court ruled in *Carpenter* that cell phone tracking violated the Fourth Amendment. "As with GPS information, the time-stamped data provides an intimate window into a person's life, revealing not only his particular movements, but through them his familial, political, professional, religious, and sexual associations," the Court explained. Yet, under the guise of public health, Massachusetts violated this principle and siphoned tax dollars to Google to monitor its citizens' movements and associations.

Two Americans challenged the constitutionality of MassNotify, alleging violations of the Fourth Amendment and the state constitution. Their complaint argued, "Conspiring with a private company to hijack residents' smartphones without the owners' knowledge or consent is not a tool that the Massachusetts Department of Public Health may lawfully employ in its efforts to combat COVID-19. Such brazen disregard for civil liberties violates both the United States and Massachusetts Constitutions, and it must stop now."

In March 2024, the District Court of Massachusetts denied the State's motion to dismiss the case. The Government had argued that cell phone users did not have a "constitutionally protected property interest in the digital storage" of their data and that the case was moot because the program was no longer in effect. The district court disagreed, holding that the plaintiffs had sufficiently alleged violations to their constitutional rights and that the Court could still grant relief related to the case. As of February 2025, the case remains in litigation, and plaintiffs have access to discovery of the State's communications relating to the program.

Google is familiar with allegations of improper tracking. In 2022, the company agreed to a record $391 million settlement with 40 states for allegedly misleading users over its location tracking programs. In 2020, Arizona filed suit against Google alleging that its citizens were "targets of a sweeping surveillance apparatus designed [by Google] to collect their behavioral data *en masse*, including data pertaining to user location." Google settled the case for $85 million. In a separate case, the Attorney General for Washington, D.C. claimed that "Google deceived consumers regarding how their location is tracked and used."

The Massachusetts app was both intrusive and ineffective. By 2021, it became clear that contact tracing had not slowed the transmission of Covid-19. In December 2021, the state announced that it was ending MassNotify after spending over $150 million on the program. Even the *New York Times* editorial page admitted in November 2020 that "there's little evidence showing that these contact tracing apps work, and they bring with them a host of questions about privacy."

The Department of Public Health explicitly violated Supreme Court precedent to implement a non-discriminatory system of mass surveillance that failed in its purported purpose. The agency enriched Silicon Valley with taxpayer funds in a clandestine scheme to strip citizens of their Fourth Amendment rights.

The Excelsior Pass

Intrusions into Americans' privacy soon became central to the Covid regime's vaccine fanaticism. Governor Andrew Cuomo used his 2021 State of the State Address to unveil plans for a digital Covid-19 vaccine passport. He dubbed it "The Excelsior Pass." "The vaccine will end the COVID crisis," Cuomo stated. "We must vaccinate 70-90% of our twenty million New Yorkers." Like other Covid efforts, the state recruited multinational corporations – including IBM and Deloitte – to assist their efforts to strip Americans of their rights.

Governor Cuomo launched a pilot program for the Excelsior Pass in March 2021. The *New York Times* called it a "magic ticket" only accessible "to people who have been vaccinated in the state." The *magic ticket* became the basis for citizens to access basic perks of civilization, including public transportation, dining, and entertainment.

Cuomo assured taxpayers that the initiative would only cost $2.5 million. It quickly ballooned to over $60 million. While the program ran 25 times over budget, the country's most powerful companies enjoyed windfalls. IBM raked in millions from New York taxpayers to maintain the health information stored in the app. Boston Consulting Group and Deloitte received nearly $30 million for their work on the program; they later received $200 million in taxpayer funds under the state's Covid "emergency" spending.

Profiteers capitalized on the opportunity as public officials welcomed the increase in state power. By August 2021, Cuomo had unveiled Excelsior Pass Plus, a program designed to expand the passport in other states and nations. Journalists later revealed that the plan predated the pandemic. The *Times Union* reported:

"New York's expanding contract with the two firms actually began...in September 2019. The broadly worded agreement covered work 'transforming or reengineering government business models and operations.' State officials agreed to spend up to $59.5 million over the ensuing five years for the services of Boston Consulting Group and Deloitte, whichever organization was better suited for the work on specific projects.

The state comptroller's office was responsible for overseeing this government spending, but it later admitted that it lost the contract during its period of remote work in response to Covid. Regardless, the groups had undoubtedly succeeded in "transforming or reengineering" the structure of civilization.

Most notably, Cuomo destroyed New Yorkers' privacy rights.

"Cuomo's dystopian program also infringes upon New Yorkers' rights to be free from unreasonable searches and seizures under the Fourth Amendment of the federal constitution," the National Civil Liberties Alliance explained. "Numerous courts have recognized that people have a reasonable expectation of privacy in their medical records, meaning that the Governor cannot compel them to divulge such information in order to participate in public life."

Cuomo's taxpayer-funded initiative violated longstanding legal precedents. For decades, federal courts of appeal have recognized that medical records "are well within the ambit of materials entitled to privacy protection." In 2000, the Fourth Circuit held that "medical treatment records...are entitled to some measure of protection from unfettered access by government officials." The Supreme Court later ruled that medical tests constituted an unconstitutional search, and "benign" motives could not "justify a departure from Fourth Amendment protections."

But the Covid vaccine passport fell under the corona-mania exemption from constitutional restraints. Medical records were publicized as an untested "emergency use" product became a prerequisite for participating in society.

Tracking the Unvaccinated

Beyond geographic tracking, the United States government secretly monitored Americans' medical records to log whether they had received Covid vaccines. Beginning in 2022, the CDC implemented a program that instructed doctors to record patients' vaccination status in an electronic medical record without their consent or knowledge.

In September 2021, a CDC committee met to discuss the use of "diagnostic codes," also known as "ICD-10" codes, to respond to "under immunization for Covid-19." These diagnostic codes are managed and compiled by the World Health Organization.

As opposed to other ICD-10 codes, the new program did not track existing illnesses or health conditions; instead, it was a measure for compliance. The coding included detailing reasons why Americans chose not to receive the vaccine. For example, the CDC created separate codes for those who remain unvaccinated "for reasons of belief."

Doctors explained that the codes offered no diagnostic benefit. "I have a hard time clinically seeing the medical indication of using them," Dr. Todd Porter, a pediatrician, told the *Epoch Times*. "We do not do this for influenza, which in the younger age groups has a higher IFR [infection fatality ratio] than COVID-19. Using these codes also disregards the contribution of natural immunity, which research evidence shows is more robust than vaccine immunity."

At the September 2021 meeting, CDC Dr. David Berglund discussed the "value" of being "able to track the unvaccinated." When asked if the codes would consider natural immunity, he said that codes would only consider citizens "fully immunized" if they received the CDC-recommended dosage of vaccines and boosters. There would be no exceptions.

The following month, Dr. Anthony Fauci and three other high-ranking US health officials held a secret meeting to discuss whether natural immunity should exempt Americans from vaccine mandates. The government cabal included US Surgeon General Vivek Murthy, CDC Director Rochelle Walensky, NIH Director Francis Collins, and White House vaccine coordinator Bechara Choucair.

At the time, the CDC recommended three shots to almost all adult Americans despite widespread research indicating that natural immunity was superior to mRNA vaccines. Walensky was a signatory to the John Snow Memorandum from October 2020, which argued that there was "no evidence for lasting protective immunity to SARS-CoV-2 following infection" despite widespread studies to the contrary.

Following the secret October 2021 meeting, US public health officials increased their vaccine recommendations without making exceptions for those with natural immunity. Within months, the United States implemented the public health apparatus's tracking program.

The CDC was straightforward in the goal of the initiative. "There is interest in being able to track people who are not immunized or only partially immunized," the agency wrote. Additionally, the insurance industry advocated for the privacy intrusion, assuring health officials that it could use the data to promote Big Pharma's liability-free products; "Creating ICD-10 codes that can be tracked via claims would provide health insurance providers key information to help increase immunization rates," wrote Danielle Lloyd, a senior vice president at America's Health, an insurance provider.

The program remained secret for nearly a year after implementation. When groups including The *Epoch Times*, Laura Ingraham, and Dr. Robert Malone revealed the tracking operation, the CDC was reluctant to answer questions.

Ten members of Congress sent a letter to CDC Director Walesnsky, writing, "we are concerned about the federal government gathering data on Americans' personal choices – data that serves no sincere purpose in treating patients' medical conditions – and how it may be used in the future."

The members continued, "The ICD system was originally intended to classify diagnoses and reasons for visiting the doctor, not to conduct surveillance on the personal medical decisions of American citizens. Given the profound uncertainty and distrust felt by many Americans toward the CDC and the medical apparatus at large, it is important for the CDC to make clear the intent and purpose of these new codes."

The CDC and Dr. Walensky declined to respond to the letter. Without a medical justification, the tracking system appears to be a compliance tool, designed at the height of vaccine mania to monitor who declined mRNA jabs and why. It was a clear violation of Fourth Amendment precedent that guarantees citizens' medical records "protection from unfettered access by government officials."

"The Architecture of Oppression"

In the opening days of the pandemic, Edward Snowden warned that governments would be reluctant to relinquish the power they would accumulate. "When we see emergency measures passed, particularly today, they tend to be sticky," Snowden said in March 2020. "The emergency tends to be expanded. Then authorities become comfortable with some new power. They start to like it."

Snowden's warnings proved prescient. *Two weeks to flatten the curve* was expanded to 1,100 days of emergency orders, and leaders reveled in their new powers. "Do you truly believe that when the first wave, this second wave, the 16th wave of the coronavirus is a long-forgotten memory, that these capabilities will not be kept?" Snowden later asked. "No matter how it is being used, what is being built is the architecture of oppression."

Even some in the US Government warned that the surveillance state would not disappear as the virus subsided. "The federal government has realized the value of the massive amounts of commercial consumer data that is freely available on the open market," Rep. Kelly Armstrong said in 2023. "Combine [the amount of data available] with the advance in technology like [artificial intelligence], facial recognition, and more, that will allow aggregation, analysis, and identification, and we are fast approaching a surveillance state with no assurances other than the promises of our government that it will not abuse this tremendous responsibility."

All evidence suggests that the government will continue to abuse the "tremendous responsibility" by partnering with Silicon Valley companies to usurp the Fourth Amendment.

Public officials used citizens' GPS data to perpetuate their power over the electorate. Voter analytics firm PredictWise boasted that it used "nearly 2 billion GPS pings" from Americans' cell phones to assign citizens scores for their "COVID-19 decree violations" and their "COVID-19 concern." The Arizona Democratic Party used these "scores" and collections of personal data to influence voters to support US Senator Mark Kelly. The firm's clients include the Democratic parties of Florida, Ohio, and South Carolina.

Politicians and government agencies repeatedly and deliberately augmented their power by tracking their citizens and thus depriving them of their Fourth Amendment rights. They then analyzed that information, assigned citizens compliance "scores," and used the spyware to manipulate voters to maintain their positions of authority.

Other countries have developed plans to make the Covid surveillance permanent.

In May 2023, the United Kingdom reached new agreements with mobile network providers to share user data that will allow the government to continue tracking population movement. The UK Health Security Agency said the information will provide insight into "behavioral changes post-pandemic...and establish a post-pandemic baseline of behavior."

Snowden warned that once authorities become comfortable with new power, "they start to like it." In Australia, Prime Minister

Scott Morrison took the unprecedented action of appointing himself minister of five departments during Covid, including the national Department of Health. Under his supervision, the Department of Health released national and state-level apps to monitor Covid infections. The programs were advertised as a means to notify people if they had been near someone who tested positive for the virus; intelligence agencies soon abused the program by "incidentally" collecting citizens' data, and law enforcement co-opted the program to investigate crimes.

Israel similarly used pandemic data programs to augment state power. The Israeli government developed tracking technologies advertised as tools to combat the spread of Covid. Using digital information, police began appearing at Israelis' homes if they were found to have violated quarantine orders. This "contact tracing" initiative then extended beyond Covid. Israel's security agency – Shin Bet – used the contact tracing technology to send threatening messages to citizens that it suspected of participating in protests against the police. By using GPS locations, the government was able to identify potential dissidents and suppress dissent.

In China, the CCP implemented QR scanners during the pandemic and insisted they would be used to monitor infections. Instead, Beijing transformed the program as the pandemic ended to restrict travel, protest, and free association.

"What COVID did was accelerate state use of these tools and that data and normalize it, so it fit a narrative about there being a public benefit," a senior researcher at an internet watchdog group told the Associated Press. "Now the question is, are we going to be capable of having a reckoning around the use of this data, or is this the new normal?"

That reckoning has yet to come. If Chinese QR codes sound like a foreign nightmare that would never come to American cities, consider how quickly the United States adopted a *Manhattan Project-level operation aimed at enforcing house arrest rules.* The Intelligence Community has long demonstrated its disregard for citizens' civil liberties or constitutional restraints. The Covid panic created an opportunity for Silicon Valley companies and the federal government to *do things they could not do before*, as Rahm Emanuel would advise. Big Tech profited from the erosion of citizens' Fourth Amendment rights. Senator Church's warning came to fruition; the Intelligence Community's capabilities were turned around on the American people, and no American had any privacy left, such is the capability to monitor everything – health records, movement, religious worship, and more. There was no place to hide.

THE ILLEGAL VACCINE
MANDATES

Initially, there was professed bipartisan opposition to Covid vaccine mandates. "No, I don't think [the shot] should be mandatory, I wouldn't demand it be mandatory," President-elect Biden told the press in December 2020. Dr. Fauci agreed. "You don't want to mandate and try and force anyone to take a vaccine. We've never done that," he explained. "It would be unenforceable and inappropriate." A few months later, Speaker of the House Nancy Pelosi echoed their sentiment. "We cannot require someone to be vaccinated," she told reporters. "That is just not what we can do. It is a matter of privacy to know who is or who isn't." In July 2021, White House Press Secretary Jen Psaki said mandates were "not the role of the federal government." She continued, "that is the role that institutions, private-sector entities, and others may take."

At first, the experimental shots remained voluntary. Despite pressure campaigns, government-sponsored propaganda, and relentless false advertising, many Americans declined the "vaccines" without becoming second-class citizens.

That changed on September 9, 2021, when President Biden announced a dramatic policy shift to compulsory vaccination. "We've been patient, but our patience is wearing thin," he told Americans as he announced mandates that applied to nearly 100 million men and women.

He demanded all federal workers and contractors be vaccinated. Additionally, he announced an "emergency rule" that would require private employers with 100 workers or more to require vaccinations or implement weekly testing protocols. Dr. Fauci suddenly announced he supported "many, many more mandates." He appeared at a conference of LGBT journalists to detail his shift in opinion. Compulsion was necessary, he explained. "You'd like to have [citizens] do it on a totally voluntary basis, but if that doesn't work, you've got to go to the alternatives." The alternative, of course, was an *involuntary* basis. The vaccine was *optional* only if people agreed to take it; then, he would reveal its true nature as a mandate.

The Covid regime got in line with the new messaging, and suddenly former opponents of mandates like Pelosi described anti-mandate views as "alarming" and "fanning the flames of dangerous disinformation." Mayor Bill de Blasio told New Yorkers, "We've got to shake people at this point and say, 'Come on now.' We tried voluntary. We could not have been more kind and compassionate...No more. Get vaccinated, or you can't work in New York City."

DNC Chair Jaime Harrison went on MSNBC to decry Republicans' "crazy" "meltdown" in response to President Biden's mandates, insisting his party was "moving forward with protecting the American people." The Democratic Party unequivocally endorsed vaccine requirements, criticizing "breathless and irresponsible talking points from Republican leaders."

In January 2022, a poll showed that 59% of Democrats favored requiring unvaccinated citizens to remain confined to their homes, 55% of Democrats supported fines for the unvaccinated, 47% of Democrats favored a government tracking system for the unvaccinated, and 45% of Democrats supported internment camps for the unvaccinated.

The 180-degree change in opinion created obvious questions. Were Biden and Fauci right when they opposed mandates, or had their concerns been "breathless and irresponsible talking points?" Could states force children to receive Covid vaccines? Were these policies merely inadvisable, or were they overreaches of government authority?

Biden's executive actions were largely unconstitutional and illegal. Mandates on children were capricious and immoral. The ramifications for local industries, government agencies, and the military were disastrous. The Covid regime shamelessly justified its actions with false claims of legal legitimacy. Each step was a calculated lie resulting in an assault on American liberties.

Can the State Mandate Sterilization?

"The principle that sustains compulsory vaccination is broad enough to cover cutting the Fallopian tubes." – Justice Oliver Wendell Holmes, Jr.

Advocates of the shots repeatedly cited a 1905 Supreme Court case that upheld a smallpox vaccine mandate. Jurists, politicians, and talking heads invoked *Jacobson v. Massachusetts* to argue that the government could require any medical program to support "public health."

In the *New York Times*, Wendy Parmet suggested that challenging *Jacobson*'s "precedent" threatened "peril for other long-accepted public health measures." CNN legal analyst Joey

Jackson called government control "the question of the pandemic, which has really made so many people suffer." He said *Jacobson* gave states the complete power to "mandate vaccinations." Former Secretary of Labor Robert Reich called the case "the essence of our society. If government can't take action on behalf of the people with regard to public health, then what good is a society?" Liberal judges agreed. Judge Frank Easterbrook of the Seventh Circuit Court of Appeals wrote, "given *Jacobson v. Massachusetts...* there can't be a constitutional problem with vaccination against SARS-CoV-2." The American Bar Association offered the glib headline "Not Breaking News: Mandatory Vaccination Has Been Constitutional for Over a Century," arguing that *Jacobson* made Covid shot requirements "One-hundred percent constitutional."

They were so self-assured that their supporters never asked them basic questions. What does *Jacobson* actually hold regarding mandates? Did the Court grant complete power to states? Could San Francisco require small doses of opiates to inoculate the population against fentanyl? Can the president require federal contractors to get the flu shot? Is that government power the "essence of our society?" Has medical freedom gone unchallenged at the Court for over a century?

Of course not, and the fanatics of the Covid vaccines misrepresented the case and deliberately omitted more recent and relevant opinions. The facts of *Jacobson* were straightforward: a smallpox epidemic arose in Massachusetts in 1902. The state required residents to get vaccinated or pay a $5 fine (about $150 in today's currency). At the time, the smallpox vaccine had been in use for 100 years and prevented transmission. Outbreaks of the disease had a case fatality rate of up to 30%. The Supreme Court, in a decision written by Justice John Marshall Harlan, upheld the vax-or-fine program three years later.

The holding, however, was not a bright-line rule in favor of mandates. Harlan explicitly denied granting governments total power to implement public health measures. He wrote that courts must overturn statutes "purporting to have been enacted to protect the public health, the public morals, or the public safety" that have "no real or substantial relation to those objects" or constitute a "plain, palpable invasion of rights."

In analyzing whether to uphold the smallpox vaccine initiative, he considered three factors: (1) whether the mandate was "arbitrary and not justified by the necessity of the case," (2) whether it went "far beyond what was reasonably required for the safety of the public," and (3) whether it was a "reasonable regulation" that had a "real and substantial relation" to the health of the citizens.

There were no demands to *follow the science* or *trust the experts*; instead, the critical analysis considered the danger posed to the overall population, alternatives to mandates, and a century of medical data.

Government agencies failed to prove each standard that Harlan cited in *Jacobson*, as explained by Gerard Bradley, a Constitutional Law professor at Notre Dame, and Dr. Harvey Risch, Professor Emeritus of Epidemiology at Yale. *Jacobson* not only didn't make mandates "100 percent constitutional;" the Supreme Court's opinion underlying the "essence of our society" suggested that Covid shot requirements were illegal. When viewed through the Court's analytical framework, the Biden administration foisted a medical experiment on Americans that was unscientific, irrational, and unconstitutional.

Arbitrary and Oppressive

The first prong of *Jacobson* considers whether the requirement is arbitrary and oppressive. Bradley and Risch argue that the mandates were irrational, thus failing to meet the legal standard. Biden's orders made no accommodations for citizens with natural immunity, and they applied to groups that faced no significant risk from the virus. "A policy requiring vaccination of people who are either already immune or of no consequence either for their own health or for spreading the infection is *arbitrary*," they write. "It is *oppressive* in inflicting a medical procedure on people who do not need it for themselves or for others."

Unlike smallpox, there were effective alternatives to vaccination, and the risk to the general public was negligible. Studies showed that natural immunity conferred protection that was up to 27 times stronger than the vaccine. Healthy children had no significant risks to Covid, yet bureaucrats across the country mandated them to receive the experimental, liability-free shots.

The punishments also offer stark contrast. In *Jacobson*, the non-compliant were issued a one-time $5 fine (approximately $150 today). They were not cast out of society, banned from restaurants, fired from their jobs, or prevented from attending school. The ramifications under the Covid regime were far more oppressive than a mere monetary penalty. Adults lost their livelihoods, children lost their educations, and citizens lost their right to attend public events.

If students had been given the option to add $150 to their overpriced tuitions, they could have reasonably evaded the shots. But this wasn't a penalty or a tax; the Covid mandates were a question of who got to engage in civil society.

Further, vaccine advocates deliberately omitted more recent decisions on medical freedom from the last century. At the very least, modern cases have updated the legal precedent for whether medical treatment is "arbitrary and oppressive."

In 1990, the Court held that citizens have a constitutional

right to refuse medical treatment, writing, "the principle that a competent person has a constitutionally protected liberty interest in refusing unwanted medical treatment may be inferred from our prior decisions. Seven years later, the Court wrote in *Washington v. Glucksberg*, "the right to refuse unwanted medical treatment is so rooted in our history, tradition, and practice as to require special protection under the Fourteenth Amendment."

That protection would be at its apex in cases when treatment is ineffective and unnecessary. But proponents of mandates deliberately omitted inconvenient legal standards in their quest to impose vaccination on the country.

The Covid regime cited *Jacobson* as if it were the North Star of American jurisprudence, a canonical case like *Brown v. Board of Education* or *Marbury v. Madison*. Like the rest of their arguments, this was entirely misleading. *Jacobson* was the basis for the Court's 1927 decision to uphold a state eugenics program in *Buck v. Bell*. The plaintiff in that case – Carrie Buck – was subject to Virginia's involuntary sterilization program, and the Court embraced *Jacobson* in its opinion.

"The principle that sustains compulsory vaccination is broad enough to cover cutting the Fallopian tubes," wrote Justice Oliver Wendell Holmes. Now, *Buck v. Bell* stands alongside *Dred Scott* and *Korematsu* in the "anti-canon" of American constitutional law. But vaccine advocates gladly utilized the same reasoning to advance its agenda: the most widespread program of forced medical care in world history.

Unreasonableness

On the second issue – whether a mandate is reasonably required for public safety – Bradley and Risch argue that the government's primary interest in vaccination is preventing the transmission of infection to others. The products not only fail this objective; the companies never tested whether they would reduce transmission before bringing them to market.

To make matters worse, mandates could be counterproductive. A March 2022 study found that the vaccine had negative efficacy in combating the virus for children under 11. The data showed that vaccinated children were 41% *more likely* to be infected than their unvaccinated peers six weeks after their shots. A later study of 96,000 California prison inmates showed that the unvaccinated had lower infection rates across all age groups than the vaccinated. A study from Pfizer showed that one in five people who received the Covid vaccines got Covid within two months.

Anecdotally, it was obvious that the shot wasn't required to promote public safety. President Biden and the media chastised Green Bay Packers Quarterback Aaron Rodgers for testing positive for Covid after not getting vaccinated. "Tell your quarterback he's got to get the vaccine," the president shouted at a Wisconsin rally. In the opinion pages of the *New York Times*, writers attacked him for "disseminating misinformation" and his "irresponsible choice not to be vaccinated." On MSNBC, Kavita Patel talked about how he put his teammates and their families at risk, calling football huddles, "literally the definition of close contact in a super spreader event." On CNN, Dr. Peter Hotez said Rodgers touted "far-right extremist views" that caused the death of "150,000 unvaccinated individuals."

None of the activists addressed how Rodgers got Covid. He hadn't attended a dinner party with RFK, Jr. or shared a steam room with anti-vaccine advocates; vaccinated teammates gave him Covid from their "breakthrough infections."

The evidence did nothing to change the regime's devotion to mRNAs.

Nearly every advocate of the vaccine got Covid after receiving the maximum allotment of shots and boosters, including Joe Biden, Jill Biden, Kamala Harris, Barack Obama, Hillary Clinton, Jen Psaki, Karine Jean-Pierre, Elizabeth Warren, Cory Booker, Merrick Garland, Antony Blinken, Albert Bourla, Lloyd Austin, Gavin Newsom, Lindsey Graham, Eric Adams, Alexandra Ocasio-Cortez, Kathy Hochul, Ted Lieu, Richard Blumenthal, Maxine Waters, Hakeem Jeffries, Rashida Tlaib, Chris Murphy, Nancy Pelosi, Liz Cheney, and more. As of February 2025, Anthony Fauci has had Covid at least three times, as has President Biden.

Their infections could not shake their faith, however, and they obediently thanked the "protection the vaccines provide." "Vaccination remains a medical requirement for our workforce," wrote Secretary of Defense Lloyd Austin in August 2022, promoting the effectiveness of boosters as he announced his positive Covid test.

By that point, the ineffectiveness of the vaccines was readily apparent. In November 2021, vaccinated English adults under 60 died at twice the rate of their unvaccinated counterparts. After achieving 90% vaccination rates, Denmark and the United Kingdom hit new highs for Covid infections in January 2022.

Third-world countries without widespread vaccine campaigns fared far better during Covid than the United States, despite the latter's access to supposedly *necessary* medical products.

Madagascar has a population of approximately 30 million. Just 8% have received any dose of the Covid vaccine. As of January 2025, the country had under 1,500 Covid-related deaths since the pandemic began. Illinois has a population of 13 million, and 79% of residents received at least 1 dose of the Covid jabs. 36,000 Illinois residents have died from Covid.

New Jersey has a population of 9.2 million, 93% of whom have received at least one dose of the Covid vaccine. Haiti has a population of 11.5 million, and just 3.5% of the island nation received a dose of the Covid vaccine. Yet New Jersey had 36,000 deaths from Covid while Haiti had just 860.

Yemen has a population of 33 million, and 3.4% received a dose of the Covid vaccine. Massachusetts has a population of under 7 million, but the state has administered nearly 17 million Covid vaccine doses. Over 95% of the state has received at least one shot. Massachusetts had over 24,000 Covid deaths while Yemen had just 2,000.

Under *Jacobson*, the shots would have to be "reasonably required for the safety of the public." Illinois had 25 times as many Covid deaths as Madagascar despite having a population of less than half its size and a vaccination rate ten times higher than the African island. New Jersey had thirty times the vaccination rate of Haiti yet suffered forty times as many Covid deaths. Massachusetts's population is one-fifth the size of Yemen, and they jabbed people at thirty times the rate. Still, the Bay State suffered twelve times as many Covid deaths as Yemen did.

The data refutes any argument that the shots were "reasonably required" for public health. The evidence directly contradicts the standards of *Jacobson*, yet no talking heads examined the different fact patterns. Vaccine fanatics repeatedly misrepresented the constitutional justification behind the smallpox shot mandate, and they ignored the stark differences in the shots.

"*Jacobson* established criteria of Safety and Efficacy that must be shown beyond all doubt, that embody the provably safe and effective use of the vaccine for decades," write Bradley and Risch. "The Covid-19 vaccines come nowhere near close to that standard." While the smallpox vaccine had been a "staple in society" for nearly a century in 1905, the FDA still classified all Covid shots as "experimental" at the time of the mandates.

And the different standards yielded predictable results. Covid shots caused injuries at 24 times the rate of ordinary scheduled vaccines, a study showed in 2021. Politicians claimed they prevented transmission, then that they prevented hospitalization, then that they prevented death. Each stage of the moving goalposts was a lie, calculated *disinformation* to induce the public to get the shots.

The prevailing orthodoxy was the opposite of the truth. *Jacobson* didn't support Covid vaccine mandates; it suggested they were unconstitutional and illegitimate. Imposing them on federal contractors, private employers, public-sector workers, and children was illegal. They failed under judicial scrutiny, and the Biden administration responded by trying to evade responsibility for their initiatives.

In June 2024, the Ninth Circuit Court of Appeals confirmed Bradley and Risch's arguments, holding that *Jacobson* was inapplicable to Covid vaccine mandates. The Court of Appeals wrote:

> "*Jacobson* held that mandatory vaccinations were rationally related to preventing the spread of smallpox. Here, however, plaintiffs allege that the vaccine does not effectively prevent spread but only mitigates symptoms for the recipient and therefore is akin to a medical treatment, not a 'traditional' vaccine. Taking plaintiffs' allegations as true at this stage of litigation, plaintiffs plausibly alleged that the COVID-19 vaccine does not effectively 'prevent the spread' of COVID-19. Thus, *Jacobson* does not apply."

That reasoning, however, meant nothing to the Biden White House, which declared absolute power to impose vaccine mandates.

The September 2021 Mandates

In September 2021, President Biden announced sweeping vaccine mandates. In total, the requirements forced one in three American adults to receive the shot or risk losing their livelihoods, a choice typically understood as coercion.

He announced plans to "sign an executive order that will now require all executive branch federal employees to be vaccinated - all. And I've signed another executive order that will require federal contractors to do the same."

The order applied to all Americans working for companies that performed any federal work, even if their roles had no connection to the government collaboration. "Simply due to the misfortune of working for a company that may have a federal contract, an American may be forced to receive a vaccine they do not want or else lose their job," a later lawsuit explained.

President Biden justified his edict under the Procurement Act, a federal law aimed to help the government enact an "economical and efficient system" for procuring services and property. He claimed, "ensuring that Federal contractors and subcontractors are adequately protected from COVID-19 will bolster economy and efficiency in Federal procurement."

But the opposite was true. The mandates risked losing access to large swaths of the labor force that didn't want to receive the shots. Biden never addressed how shrinking the labor pool would promote efficiency; when his administration was forced to defend his parchment declaration in court, the orders could not withstand judicial scrutiny.

In December 2021, a judge blocked the mandate for federal contractors from going into effect. The mandate "goes far beyond addressing administrative and management issues," wrote District Court Judge Stan Baker. It "works as a regulation of public health, which is not clearly authorized under the Procurement Act." Baker explained that the mandate created economic burdens, not efficiencies. Biden not only lacked a proper justification; he was effectuating the opposite of his professed intention. Judge Baker issued a nationwide injunction that prevented the order from going into effect.

The following month, another District Court Judge blocked the mandates. "[The orders] amount to a presidential mandate that all federal employees consent to vaccination against Covid-19 or lose their jobs," wrote Judge Jeffrey V. Brown. "The President's authority is not that broad." It was a "bridge too far" for the White House "with a stroke of a pen or without the input of congress, to require millions of federal employees to undergo a medical procedure as a condition of their employment," he explained.

The White House appealed the injunction, relying on Biden's "economy and efficiency" justification. The 11th US Circuit Court of Appeals held arguments on the case that summer and upheld Judge Backer's injunction in August 2022. The panel concluded that President Biden "likely exceeded his authority" under the Procurement Act.

Texas Attorney General Ken Paxton led states in filing suits against the Biden administration demanding the invalidation of the September 2021 mandates. In May 2023, the White House announced the end of its vaccination requirements for federal employees and contractors, withdrawing the requirements before the case could reach the Supreme Court.

"Joe Biden egregiously exceeded his authority in his attempt to force all federal contractors to be vaccinated or face losing their jobs," Paxton said in response. "It is beneath contempt for a President to threaten a worker's ability to feed their family to achieve compliance with his mandates."

Unwilling to undergo another potential judicial defeat, the White House withdrew its requirements, bringing the regime's mandate policy full circle. The federal government had returned to Biden's initial stance. Mandates were no longer "the role of the federal government," as Jen Psaki had explained less than two years earlier. It again became "the role that institutions, private-sector entities, and others may take."

OSHA

Congress created OSHA – the 1970 Occupational Safety and Health Act –to "prevent workers from being killed or seriously harmed at work." The Act has led to workplace-specific protections like regulating exposure to asbestos, preventing trenches from caving in, and requiring licenses for hazardous jobs.

Just as Biden attempted to warp the Procurement Act to support his vaccine crusade, the White House sought to transform OSHA from a workplace protection program to a bludgeon to impose government policy on the private sector. President Biden's executive order invoked OSHA to require all businesses with 100 or more employees to implement requirements for vaccines, testing, and masking.

White House Press Secretary Jen Psaki called the policies "critical to our nation's COVID-19 response." The Department of Justice argued that the programs were necessary to prevent "serious health consequences" from unvaccinated workers. The order applied to more than two-thirds of the private sector, accounting for over 80 million Americans.

Businesses and states filed lawsuits, arguing that the program exceeded the scope of President Biden's authority. The President could not repurpose OSHA to two-thirds of the workforce, they maintained. They argued that Biden's theory would give the Department of Labor "limitless, unprecedented power over American industry by allowing the agency to target dangers that exist in workplaces only because they exist in the world at large." In January 2022, their case reached the Supreme Court.

The Court held that Biden's mandate was illegal. "The Act [OSHA] empowers the Secretary of Labor to set workplace safety standards, not broad public health measures," the majority wrote. But Covid was not a workplace safety issue – it spreads "at home, in schools, during sporting events, and everywhere else that people gather. That kind of universal risk is no different from the day-to-day dangers that all face from crime, air pollution, or any number of communicable diseases." It was illegitimate to use a "general risk" to warp OSHA to the President's demands to institute a "significant encroachment into the lives – and health – of a vast number of employees," the Court wrote.

In a concurring opinion, Justice Gorsuch wrote that local authorities "possess considerable power to regulate public health" while federal powers remain "limited and divided." Without those limits, he argued, "emergencies would never end and the liberties our Constitution's separation of powers seeks to preserve would amount to little."

Of course, the explicit aim of the executive mandates was to circumvent the separation of powers. As Dr. Fauci tellingly explained, voluntary compliance was insufficient to meet their demands. It was a program of mandatory conformity, and President Biden was unwilling to cede public health power to local governments. In September 2021, he infamously told the unvaccinated, "We've been patient, but our patience is wearing thin. And your refusal has cost all of us." It was his impatience, and resulting intolerance, that led him to issue his broad and illegal mandates.

The Covid regime denounced the Court's decision. House Speaker Nancy Pelosi told the press, "the Court has chosen to ignore the science and the law by preventing the Administration from keeping Americans safe in the workplace." Fauci later told the *New York Times* that opposition to mandates was part of a "smoldering anti-science feeling, a divisiveness that's palpable politically in this country."

The White House quietly withdrew its OSHA mandates two weeks later. The agency later pretended the whole episode never happened. OSHA head Douglas Parker testified to Congress "We didn't threaten anyone, and we didn't demand that anyone be fired." Their tyrannical diktats were unable to withstand judicial scrutiny, yet they refused to admit error. The White House described how "President Biden marshalled a wartime effort" to increase vaccination rates. Approximately 30 million Americans received the vaccine within ten weeks of his first mandate. The effort had been illegal, but it had been successful.

Vaccinating Children

In just 8 months, Dr. Anthony Fauci went from publicly opposing all Covid vaccine mandates to suggesting they should be imposed upon schoolchildren. "I believe that mandating vaccines for children to appear in school is a good idea," he told CNN in August 2021. He compared it to the polio vaccine and urged school districts to force parents to jab their children for a disease that posed no risk to them.

Like the discussion surrounding *Jacobson*, public officials and talking heads acted as if this were uncontroversial. If the anointed Tony Fauci had called for it, then the orders must be worshiped. Again, however, the mandates couldn't withstand simple scrutiny.

Jenin Younes, an attorney with the New Civil Liberties Alliance, explained in the *Wall Street Journal*, "Forced Covid vaccination for kids is unlawful." She addressed Fauci's comparison to "standard childhood shots" like polio and diphtheria, explaining that "those decades-old vaccines have gone through the full FDA testing regime" while "the Covid vaccine [had] received only emergency-use authorization" (EUA) for children in fall 2021.

Federal law prohibits patients from being forced, coerced, or pressured into taking EUA products. Requiring children to get shots in order to participate in public life or attend school was the "antithesis of free and informed consent is therefore unlawful," Younes argued.

Those rather basic legal principles were lost in the hysteria of Covid. Like their years of lost youth and education, Fauci and the White House proposed sacrificing children's freedoms to advance their agendas. Younes concluded her article, "Let's not make forced vaccination of young children, which is unconstitutional and illegal under federal law, the next way in which we disregard their interests to mollify adults' irrational fears."

But the regime plowed ahead. In October 2021, California became the first state to announce that Covid vaccines would be required for students once it had FDA approval. "The state already requires that students are vaccinated against viruses that cause measles, mumps, and rubella – there's no reason why we wouldn't do the same for COVID-19," Gavin Newsom explained as he celebrated his new mandate. Washington, D.C., Detroit, and other areas announced similar plans.

Apparently siloed in a bubble of coronamania, lawmakers were shocked to find parents resisted their orders as they refused to vaccinate their children for a disease that didn't harm them. In the District of Columbia, the government announced that it would postpone its mandate when nearly half of DC public school students remained unvaccinated after the deadline to get the shots passed. Mayor Eric Adams dropped vaccine requirements for New York City student-athletes when vaccination rates hovered around 50%. California courts found that school mandates in Los Angeles and San Diego were illegal, delaying the enforcement of Newsom's vaccine campaign into the 2022-2023 school year. In February 2023, California quietly dropped its Covid mandate for students. The Newsom Administration leaked the news to the press without any accompanying announcement or explanation.

"Children have a right to bodily autonomy and to refuse unnecessary medical treatment, which their parents exercise on their behalf," Younes wrote in her argument. "The government can't conscript them as guinea pigs or vessels to protect adults." Parents' exercise of those rights halted the mandates. As of 2023, approximately two-thirds of American children remained "unvaccinated" according to the CDC. Just 7% of children had received recommended boosters. Even in Democratic-leaning areas, fewer than one in eight children were "up-to-date" with their recommended Covid shots. Mass resistance, rather than the rule of law, withstood the tyranny of the regime.

Downstream Consequences

Not only were the means illegal, but the ends were disastrous. At least 8,000 troops were kicked out of the US military for declining to take the Covid vaccine. In 2022, the military reported zero Covid deaths among active troops, but Secretary of Defense Lloyd Austin insisted on continuing the mandates.

He was clear in his orders. In December 2022, the press asked who was responsible for the policies. Austin responded, "I'm the guy." He added, "I support continuation of vaccinating the troops." The Pentagon continued to force healthy soldiers to choose between the vaccine or expulsion from the military, regardless of prior infection, until senators intervened.

In January 2023, Senators Rand Paul and Ted Cruz added requirements to the National Defense Authorization Act that forced the Defense Department to repeal its mandate. The Pentagon did not concede its irrationality; however, it later announced that it would not offer back pay to any troops discharged for failure to comply with the mandate.

Lloyd Austin gloated that he had forced soldiers to choose between an experimental vaccine and their service to their country. In a memo, he announced that he was "deeply proud of the Department's work to combat the coronavirus disease," adding that his edicts "will have a lasting legacy in the many lives we saved."

But Austin has never had to answer for the cost-benefit analysis of his decisions. At the same time that the military hit historic shortfalls in its recruitment efforts, his mandate cut the strength of American forces. The purported benefit was increasing the number of troops who took an ineffective vaccine for a virus that did not threaten their health. In January 2025, President Trump reinstated service members who were fired for refusing the vaccine. His executive order described the act as "correcting an injustice," citing that "in spite of the scientific evidence, the Biden Administration discharged healthy service members—many of whom had natural immunity and dedicated their entire lives to serving our country—for refusing the COVID vaccine. Government redress of these wrongful dismissals is overdue."

But the damage, in large part, had already taken effect, and the disruptions were not limited to the military. After President Biden's vaccine orders in September 2021, Southwest announced a vaccine requirement for all staff and pilots. The Southwest Airlines Pilots Association filed suit to stop the mandate. Two days later, the airline cancelled 1,800 flights over Columbus Day weekend, blaming bad weather and staff shortages.

As the mandate continued, so did delays, cancellations, and staffing shortages. In June 2022, 1,300 Southwest employees picketed the Dallas Airport to protest the vaccine requirement. "Why are we having a staffing shortage?" asked Tim Bogart, a Southwest pilot. "I believe it's because of the COVID vaccines."

The country is less efficient and less safe; citizens experience a continuing decline in quality of life; children are less healthy, and vaccine injuries permanently damaged families. Those struggles can be directly tied to the top-down mandates that took over nearly every sector of American life. They were illogical, immoral, and illegal; and the most influential members of our society – from the legal world, the media landscape, and the levers of government power – facilitated and guaranteed their implementation.

THE COVID CASTE SYSTEM: HOW RADICALS OVERTURNED EQUALITY OF THE LAW

In normal times, Americans would hear Daniel Uhlfelder barking from a street corner about end times. "Just keep walking," they'd tell their kids as they caught glimpses of his signs predicting rapture. People might have different approaches to getting him help – rehab, a social support system, family intervention – but nobody would treat him as a public policy advocate. But 2020's Ides of March were not normal times, however, so lunacy elevated Uhlfelder to adoring media coverage and a political platform.

Beginning in March 2020, Uhfelder, a Florida attorney, dedicated himself to shaming parents who brought their children to local beaches. He dressed as the Grim Reaper, covered head to toe in a black cloak with a scythe in his hand. Instead of questioning his sanity or explaining that sunlight killed the virus, liberal news outlets celebrated the unhinged lawyer.

"It's a macabre plea to beachgoers to stay home," CNN wrote alongside a picture of Uhlfelder standing in front of a beach umbrella covered in his signature costume. He handed out body bags and warned beachgoers that venturing outside would kill them and their loved ones. "You are inviting death and disease to walk amongst you," he scolded them. Saturday Night Live, Vice News, and the Daily Show covered him, celebrating rather than mocking his efforts. "If we don't take measures to control things, this virus is going to get really, really out of control," he warned.

The New Yorker published a glowing profile on the Sunshine State's Grim Reaper. "I'm not a liberal," he said. "I'm logical." He compared his publicity tour to his family's experience in the Holocaust. "My grandfather escaped Nazi Germany as a teenager. His whole family was incinerated in gas chambers," he said. "It was always ingrained in my head: 'You can sit around and bitch and whine, but what are you going to do about it?'" To honor the memory of the Holocaust, Uhlfelder responded to national fear by scapegoating political opponents and urging the suspension of their liberties.

Uhlfelder held higher aspirations than terrorizing local families. He used his publicity to open the Make My Day PAC, a political action committee supporting pro-lockdown Democrats. Later that year, he launched an unsuccessful campaign for Florida Attorney General, receiving 400,000 votes.

Despite his anti-science hysteria, the media gave Uhlfelder far more favorable coverage than Ron DeSantis could ever hope to receive. *The New Yorker* published his Holocaust invocation without any blowback. Months later, the press called Robert F. Kennedy, Jr. "anti-Semitic" and "offensive" for mentioning Nazi Germany in a speech decrying totalitarianism. By July, CNN welcomed Uhlfelder as a commentator on mask mandates. "Unfortunately, when I started this work in March, I had a bad belief that this was going to get really bad," he said. "[DeSantis] needs to issue a mask order because masks work."

But there was a notable carveout to Uhlfelder's attitude toward public gatherings. On May 26, 2020, he posted photos of his continued efforts to shame his neighbors into sitting alone inside. He even had multiple costumes, incorporating a hazmat suit into his outfit rotation. One week later, he celebrated millions of citizens gathering across the country after the death of George Floyd. He personally attended BLM rallies in Florida and endorsed marches in New York, San Francisco, and Chicago.

A country with 300 million people will always have narcissistic, hypocritical lunatics like Uhfelder; more alarming, however, was how he represented the country's ruling class in those months.

Equality of law was overturned in favor of a Covid caste system. The lockdowns, the edicts, the house arrests, the arbitrary deprivations of liberty, the capricious assaults on constitutional rights, and the irrational executive orders were all reserved for citizens with the wrong political persuasion. Small businesses shuttered amid "nonessential" decrees while Planned Parenthood remained open. Protests against lockdowns resulted in arrests while governors joined thousands in "anti-racism" marches. Common citizens couldn't eat in a restaurant or get their hair cut, but the powerful remained immune from the orders of the Covid regime.

There were at least three factors that demarcated the two-tiered system of law that infected the United States in 2020: profession, ideology, and power. First, CISA divided the workforce into "essential" and "nonessential" categories that allowed the world's most powerful corporations to continue their operations while small businesses and churches were subject to lockdowns. Second, the architects of lockdowns based their enforcement on whether groups held proper political beliefs. Socially political movements like Black Lives Matter earned an exemption from their totalitarianism. Third, governors, bureaucrats, and mayors flouted their own regulations and enjoyed the freedoms that they denied to their fellow citizens.

It was more than hypocrisy; it was despotism. The abolition of the American Creed led to suffering for the most vulnerable and immense riches for the powerful. It was not mere selfishness; it was callous cruelty. Suddenly, American citizens were subject to a political regime that suppressed their longest-standing liberties if they failed to comply with the latest ideological trends. Their children, their businesses, and their freedoms suffered as ostensible public servants advanced political agendas.

The Black Lives Matter Exception

Michigan Governor Gretchen Whitmer was one of the country's most ardent enforcers of lockdowns. Her citizens lost their basic rights to petition government, travel, and assemble. In April 2020 , she called protests against her stay-at-home order "racist and misogynistic." She threatened that the demonstrations would make it "likelier" that the lockdowns would continue.

But Whitmer's tune changed when "anti-racism" protestors and rioters arrived in Detroit in June. She greeted them with enthusiasm, marching side-by-side with the group. Whitmer brazenly violated her executive orders, which required "social distancing measures...including remaining at least six feet from people." She was clear that politics drove her decision to march arm-in-arm with her voting bloc. "Elections matter," she shouted from a microphone. "We cannot be defeated."

Like Uhlfelder, Whitmer combined dictatorial arrogance with cognitive dissonance. At the time of her BLM political rally, she threatened political opponents with 90 days in jail if they violated her stay-at-home order. Thousands gathered in Grand Rapids,

Kalamazoo, and the State Capitol for BLM rallies, but Whitmer refrained from punishing the lawbreakers. As political allies of the administration, they were not subject to the edicts that applied to the broader citizenry.

Illinois took a similar approach. When asked about the ramifications for violating stay-at-home orders, Chicago Mayor Lori Lightfoot told reporters, "We will arrest. That should never happen because people – meaning you – have to comply." Governor J.B. Pritzker was similarly stern in his house arrest demands. "All public and private gatherings of any number of people occurring outside a single household or living unit are prohibited," he decreed. For non-favored citizens, it was the most extreme form of totalitarianism: *all* gatherings at *any* place with *any* persons were banned. As was "all travel, including, but not limited to, travel by automobile, motorcycle, scooter, bicycle, train, plane, or public transit."

Illinois's lockdown enforcement continued into the summer. In late May, Chicago Police issued warnings that they would arrest and fine anyone who biked on outdoor trails, even if riding alone. When a local group of Republicans planned an outdoor Fourth of July picnic, Pritzker went to court to enforce lockdowns. But none of these standards applied to Black Lives Matter.

"We want people to come and express their passion," Mayor Lightfoot told reporters weeks after she scolded citizens that they "had to comply." Thousands of protestors gathered in cities across the state, with looters inflicting over $100 million in damage. Unlike public policy aimed at solo bike rides, there was no concern for viral transmission.

Civil liberties hinged on political persuasion under the governor's regime. Like Whitmer, Pritzker participated in a march with hundreds of activists in June. In the ensuing months, he banned the Illinois Republican Party from holding rallies in the lead-up to the 2020 presidential election. It was clear viewpoint discrimination – the Governor marched alongside a political group he supported and banned events for a party he opposed. Local media was largely silent as the governor suspended political freedom under an irrational public health excuse. Without explaining how his marches differed in safety, he argued that curbing the activities of his opponents was "necessary" to prevent the spread of Covid.

In November 2020, President Biden won the election, and the standards for political demonstrations shifted again. The obese Pritzker marched through Chicago with thousands of supporters. Like Black Lives Matter, the Democratic Party enjoyed an exemption from the lockdown measures. "It's clear the governor keeps one set of rules for the people in politically advantageous photo ops and another for the rest of Illinois," Republican Party Chairman Tim Schneider said in response.

Mayor Lightfoot joined thousands in celebrating President Biden's election. "It's a great day for our country," she shouted to the crowd. Her political allies filled the streets around her, packed shoulder to shoulder. Five days later, Lightfoot returned to authoritarian impulse. "You must cancel the normal Thanksgiving plans," she demanded. According to Lightfoot, it was simply too dangerous to interact with "guests that do not live in your immediate household."

Governor Cuomo implemented a similar two-tier legal system in the Empire State. "How many people have to die before the people ignoring social distancing get that they have a responsibility?" He asked on Twitter in April. "One person sneezes – another person gets intubated...STAY HOME. SAVE LIVES." Just weeks after he shut down church pastors for hosting drive-in sermons, BLM protestors were immune from law enforcement.

In neighboring New Jersey, Governor Phil Murphy embraced the double standards. Murphy was one of the strictest enforcers of lockdowns beginning in March 2020. That spring, New Jersey police charged citizens for crimes including:

- "Congregating without maintaining a distance of 6FT, and without a destination, in violation of the Governor's order;"
- "Failing to obey a governor's Ex. Order by taking part in non-essential travel & failing to social distance;"
- and "standing in violation of Governor's orders."

When asked about Murphy's enforcement of Corona-law, an attorney from the ACLU of New Jersey remarked, "It's a little breathtaking, the scope."

But when thousands of Black Lives Matter protestors gathered in Newark, there were no similar citations. Murphy was clear: the application of the law depended on whether he found the group's cause morally sufficient. "I'll probably get lit up by everyone who owns a nail salon in the state," he said in June. "But it's one thing to protest what day nail salons are opening, and it's another to come out in peaceful protest, overwhelmingly, about somebody who was murdered right before our eyes."

Later that summer, his police arrested owners of a local gym for operating their business in defiance of his orders and homeowners for hosting a pool party without social distancing. The gym owners hadn't flipped over cars or torched police vehicles like BLM's "peaceful" protestors in Trenton, and the pool party didn't descend into gang violence like the "anti-racism" movement in Atlantic City. Their crime was their ideology.

Unelected ideologues were not immune from the hypocrisy.

Former CDC Director Tom Frieden warned in a *Washington Post* op-ed that violating stay-at-home orders and lockdowns could "overwhelm health-care facilities, killing doctors, nurses, patients, and others." Protests against shuttering businesses and schools was akin to mass homicide to Frieden, but there was a policy exception for the George Floyd riots. "People can protest peacefully AND work together to stop Covid," he insisted.

Thirteen hundred public health workers signed an open letter that explained why the "anti-racism" protests should be exempt from the restrictions that other groups faced. "Protests against systemic racism, which foster the disproportionate burden of COVID-19 on Black communities and also perpetuates police violence, must be supported." Meanwhile, protests against stay-at-home orders "not only oppose public health interventions but are also rooted in white nationalism and run contrary to respect for Black lives," they explained. They did away with any veneer of medical expertise. They slandered their opponents as neo-Nazis, celebrated their allies, and insisted liberty depended on political beliefs.

"Freedom for me, but not for thee, has no place under our Constitution," U.S. Circuit Judge James Ho later explained. But that was exactly the double standard that politicians and health officials applied through the summer of 2020. Dr. Peter Hotez, a regular MSNBC contributor and an outspoken supporter of the Covid regime, chastised protests against mandates and lockdowns as "just a fresh coat of paint for the anti-vaccine movement in America, and an exploitative means for them to try to remain relevant." But when thousands gathered for BLM marches, Hotez defended the protestors as righteous opposition against "structural racism."

In June 2020, the American Public Health Association declared, "Racism is a public health crisis." Their members used that slogan to justify their support of BLM gatherings after months of promoting house arrests. The American Academy of Pediatrics, the American Medical Association, and the American College of Physicians issued similar proclamations, as did groups at Harvard, Georgetown, and Cornell and local governments in California, Wisconsin, and Maryland.

Self-professed experts in virology turned out to be ideological fanatics, shameless in their pursuit of power. The "American Creed" – the Jeffersonian principle that all men are created equal and must be treated equally before the law – was overturned in favor of blunt-force partisan politics. For over two centuries, the Constitution strove to be agnostic to the content of one's character or ideas. When Justice Scalia described the First Amendment as "an equal protection clause for ideas," he meant that its guarantees were not subject to political favoritism. But petty tyrants overturned that tradition, implementing a two-tiered system of justice that rewarded allies of the regime and punished its opponents.

Sanctimonious Sadism

Repeatedly, politicians were caught violating their Covid orders. Edicts concerning masking, travel, and work applied to the general citizenry, not elected officials.

This wasn't harmless hypocrisy. They weren't caught having a beer at the Mothers Against Drunk Driving fundraiser or jaywalking in the town square. It wasn't Ted Cruz going to Mexico during a snowstorm or even Marion Barry smoking crack. It was despotism. Children were kept out of the classroom. Their IQs plummeted, and their language skills may never recover from the effects of masking. Globally, lockdowns and Covid supply chain disruptions killed 10,000 children per month from hunger.

Businesses shut down permanently. Their owners lost their livelihood and lifetimes of work, often leading to substance abuse and mental anguish. Nearly everyone was forced to skip routine health appointments. Ten million Americans missed cancer screenings in the first fourteen months of the pandemic, and 46% of chemotherapy patients missed treatments. Churches were prohibited from opening. Their congregations were left with nowhere to turn for guidance in a spiritual crisis. Millions of people were left to die alone as stay-at-home orders prevented loved ones from visiting. Their final days were spent in solitude with no chance to say goodbye. Those responsible for this suffering insisted it was to promote health.

Supposed public servants exempted themselves from the hell that they imposed. They were unremorseful and offered insultingly stupid excuses. It was an exercise in humiliation, a public display of dominance and submission. While millions suffered, they enjoyed the freedoms that they stole from the citizenry.

In November 2020, Wisconsin Senator Tammy Baldwin continued her advocacy for lockdowns and business closures. "Don't host or go to gatherings with people outside your household," she scolded citizens before Thanksgiving." Three weeks earlier, however, she used government money to fly from Wisconsin to New York City to visit her lover for a long weekend.

The day she left for her vacation, she tweeted: "We have a raging #COVID19 outbreak in Wisconsin and across the country. This pandemic is getting worse and we need to start working together to contain it so we can get our economy on the right track and move forward." Not only was Baldwin ignoring the tyranny that she supported, she used taxpayer money to fund her duplicity.

In California, Governor Newsom exemplified the nationwide trend of sanctimony and hypocrisy. Politico explained: "Newsom has regularly implored Californians to remain vigilant by wearing masks, avoiding mixing with other households and practicing social distancing, repeating a mantra that individual behavior can make a difference."

Newsom's office chided Californians in October: "Going out to eat with members of your household this weekend? Don't forget to keep your mask on in between bites." The following month, he issued warnings against traveling for Thanksgiving or meeting with other households.

"Wear your mask. Physically distance. Do not let your guard down," Newsom tweeted on November 12. Later that week, the *San Francisco Chronicle* reported that the Governor had attended a birthday dinner at Napa Valley's French Laundry, one of the most expensive restaurants in the world, for a state lobbyist. When the news broke, the host released a statement insisting, "This was a small, intimate 12-person dinner held outdoors with family and a few close friends."

But that was a lie. Los Angeles's local Fox team obtained photos of the dinner. There were no masks, no social distancing, and they were inside. They hadn't even remembered to put on their mask *in between bites.* They had *let their guard down.* While the rest of the state lived under continued lockdowns, Newsom's children attended private school in person, and he enjoyed dinner with the company of like-minded plutocrats. The CEO of the California Medical Association and health lobbyists joined Newsom at the party. This wasn't old-fashioned hypocrisy like a "family values" candidate with a sleazy affair; Newsom had taken dictatorial control of his state and refused to abide by the edicts that he imposed.

Newsom's habit of lying and disregarding Covid law was widespread in California. San Francisco banned hair salons from operating beginning in March 2020. Those rules didn't apply to Nancy Pelosi, who had her assistant message a stylist that she needed an appointment. Disregarding local law, the Speaker of the House opened a shuttered hair salon for a blow-out. She neglected to wear a mask despite her repeated orders for other Americans to obey government demands.

After months of serving a regime that banned business owners from earning a living, Pelosi insisted on special treatment. "It was a slap in the face that she went in," the salon owner said. "She feels that she can just go and get her stuff done while no one else can go in, and I can't work."

Like Newsom, Pelosi's office instinctively lied when confronted with her hypocrisy. "The Speaker always wears a mask and complies with local COVID requirements," her spokesman told Fox News, despite photographic evidence to the contrary.

Chicago Mayor Lori Lightfoot was more forthcoming about her decision to get her hair cut despite banning salons via her stay-at-home order. She told the press that her appearance was just more important than others. "I'm the public face of this city," she explained. "I'm on national media and I'm out in the public eye."

In February 2022, Los Angeles still maintained a mask mandate under the orders of Mayor Eric Garcetti. "You MUST wear a mask," the Los Angeles County website guidance explained. Students of all ages were required to wear masks in school, but the rules did not apply to Mayor Garcetti. On February 13, 2022, Los Angeles hosted the Super Bowl. Fans received a complimentary KN95 mask upon entry, and the city required them to show proof of vaccination. Garcetti sat above the crowd in a private box with Governor Newsom, San Francisco Mayor London Breed, and celebrities including Rob Lowe and Magic Johnson.

Johnson posted photos from the evening, and none of the

politicians wore the masks that they mandated. Newsom smiled in a Twitter post, barefaced with his back to the group's private bar and dining. Garcetti posed with Johnson and Breed, celebrating maskless as the hometown LA Rams won the Super Bowl.

When confronted with their violation of the laws they imposed, the autocrats lied. "I wore my mask the entire game," insisted Garcetti. "When people ask for a photograph, I hold my breath." As children were forced to suffer under his regime for a virus that didn't harm them, Garcetti instinctively fibbed. It was more than poor leadership. He celebrated that the rules didn't apply to him, and he had such little respect for his citizens that he expected them to accept that he had mastered virology by superhuman control of his respiratory system.

Newsom offered a similar excuse. "I was very judicious yesterday…In my left hand is the mask, and I took a photo," he said. "The rest of the time I wore it, as we all should."

Flaunting capricious edicts was not reserved for California politicians. Philadelphia Mayor Jim Kenney banned all indoor dining in Philadelphia in the summer of 2020 and required residents to wear face masks and socially distance. "Let's not push the envelope," he told reporters on August 20, 2022. "I beg you to follow the rules." Kenney was clear that he would not tolerate any insubordination. "We will be quick to close restaurants," he warned.

The following week, Kenney went to Maryland to enjoy a maskless indoor dinner without social distancing. *Not pushing the envelope* was reserved for the proles, not his family vacationing on the Chesapeake Bay. When photographs of the dinner surfaced online, one Philadelphia restaurateur responded, "I guess all your press briefings and your narrative of unsafe indoor dining don't apply to you. Thank you for clearing it all up for us tonight."

While chefs and waiters lost their jobs for obeying his fiat, Kenney used his resources to avoid the ramifications of his regime.

Michigan Governor Gretchen Whitmer jailed restaurant owners for violating her executive orders. Marlena Pavlos-Hackney, a pizzeria owner, spent 4 nights in jail and paid a $15,000 fine in February 2021 for violating the state's Covid restrictions. Three months later, photos emerged of Whitmer with dozens of friends at an East Lansing restaurant. Her executive order required social distancing and limited crowd gatherings to 6 people, but it only applied to common citizens like Pavlos-Hackney who needed to earn a living. Whitmer and her like-minded friends were exempt. "Because we were all vaccinated, we didn't stop to think about it," she told the press.

Whitmer offered no remorse for implementing a two-tiered police state. "If I have to face penalties which I went through…I think she should face the same penalties," Pavlos-Hackney told Fox News. "We the people, we are all equal."

Whitmer later joined other Democratic governors in ignoring their Corona-law to attend President Biden's inauguration. At the time, Whitmer criminalized all outdoor public gatherings with "more than 25 people," regardless of masking and social distancing protocols. That same order had been used to issue thousands of dollars in fines to store owners and bars. This did not stop Whitmer from attending the inauguration with thousands of fellow Democrats and posting photos from the event. Democratic governors from Pennsylvania and New Jersey also attended the event despite their restrictions limiting gatherings and traveling.

Other officials did not have to break the law to demonstrate their disregard for their despotism. In Virginia, Alexandria City Public Schools superintendent Gregory Hutchings oversaw a $300 million budget and 15,000 students. Under his leadership, Alexandria City Public Schools did not fully reopen until August 2021.

Hutchings bemoaned the "dual pandemic of Covid-19 and systemic racism" that he and his colleagues endured. "WE ARE ON AN ANTI-RACIST JOURNEY," he declared on his school-sponsored podcast, celebrating his opportunity to rename schools. On their first day of Zoom learning for the 2020 school year, Hutchings told students, "we must acknowledge our racial inequities."

But Hutchings failed to live up to his egalitarian diatribes. While he kept 15,000 students out of the classroom that fall, he transferred his daughter to a private school that conducted in-person learning. When the press confronted him over this decision, he insisted that the choice was "very personal" and "not taken lightly."

Governor Newsom also sent his children to private school for in-person learning while almost all California public schools remained shuttered. When asked to explain himself, he deferred to local districts and the teachers' unions.

Schools in the Bay Area remained closed through Spring 2021 at the behest of Matt Meyer, president of the Berkeley Federation of Teachers. Meyer insisted that returning to the classroom was too "unsafe." It was later revealed that he sent his daughter to private school for in-person learning. When his hypocrisy was exposed, Meyer offered no remorse; instead, he lashed out at reporters, calling the story a violation of his daughter's privacy and "very inappropriate."

The people responsible for serving American children acted with brazen hypocrisy and self-interest. Teachers cancelled Zoom classes to attend destination weddings after claiming their fear of Covid prevented them from teaching in the classroom. Randi Weingarten and teachers' unions lobbied the CDC to keep schools closed. Stacey Abrams and other candidates smiled for campaign photos at schools while forcing students to remain masked.

They did this while children suffered. The average American student fell six months behind in math due to school closures. Poorer students lost two-and-a-half years of learning. The decreased math scores were the largest drop in recorded history. Unsurprisingly, school closures led to adverse mental health symptoms including distress, anxiety, and huge surges in unhealthy physical activities, including higher screen time and lower rates of exercise.

The End of the American Creed

Jefferson's American Creed survived the Civil War and the Civil Rights Movement. Leaders like Lincoln and MLK embraced it for their causes – holding that they sought to "cash a check" on the nation's foundational promise.

That tradition ended in 2020. Supposedly serious people acted as insane as a man dressed in a grim reaper costume at the Florida beach. They wielded their power capriciously, weaponizing the legal system against political opponents. They lived in luxury while denying basic freedoms to their citizens. Their grandiose moralizing became a thin façade for their overwhelming incompetence. Their decadence could not be disturbed by the plight of their citizens.

When their lies became public, they demonstrated unrepentant arrogance. They considered themselves beyond reproach. Their media, their police departments, their "public health experts," and their corporate donors were unwavering. They cared about power, not democratic accountability or constitutional norms.

In doing so, the Covid response unwound the social fabric and destroyed the foundational principles of the American legal system.

Selling the Seventh Amendment: How the Vaccines Became Compulsory and You Lost Your Right to Sue Big Pharma

"Glory Days End for Pharmaceuticals," the *New York Times* declared in February 1985. The article cited growing legal liabilities as an indication that "the big drug companies have suddenly found themselves mired in the same sort of troubles that have plagued less-glamorous industries for years." The *Times* reported, "Inevitably some [companies] will face staggering liabilities and lengthy court cases on approved drugs that later turn into flops."

Later that year, a government study funded by vaccine manufacturers, the US Army, and the Rockefeller Foundation recommended a national program to transfer the cost of vaccine liabilities from Big Pharma to American taxpayers through a "no-fault national program."

One year after the *New York Times* warned that legal liabilities threatened Pharma's "glory days," Wyeth and other pharmaceutical companies lobbied Congress to pass the 1986 National Childhood Vaccine Injury Act (the "NCVIA"), which codified the recommendations of the Merck-funded government study into law. Taxpayers have assumed the burden of the liabilities from the profiting manufacturers' products ever since.

In retrospect, the glory days hadn't even started for pharmaceuticals in 1985. The childhood vaccination schedule exploded from three recommended vaccines (DTP, MMR, and polio) to 72 shots. For nearly 40 years, the Government has been able to mandate the shots, guaranteeing billions of dollars in revenue for Merck, Pfizer, and other drug manufacturers, while transferring the cost of their products, including settlements for hundreds of millions of dollars for vaccine injuries, onto the taxpayer.

How did the most powerful companies in the country end up with a liability shield for their most lucrative products? For four decades, the pharmaceutical industry dedicated hundreds of billions of dollars to lobbying, public relations, and media manipulation. The efforts successfully purchased the obedience of the press corps, windfalls from the federal government, and an extra-constitutional status above the citizens who fund their operations.

During the Covid response, Big Pharma enjoyed its most profitable years while the rest of the world suffered under lockdowns and school closures. Pfizer's annual revenue jumped from $3.8 billion in 1984 to a record $100 billion in 2022, including $57 billion from Covid products. From 2020 to 2022, Moderna's revenue increased by over 2,000 percent. BioNTech made over $30 billion from the Covid-19 vaccine in just two years. Its profit margin exceeded 75 percent. In 2023, the ten largest pharmaceutical companies had a combined market cap of $2.8 trillion, larger than the GDP of France.

Federal purchases of Pfizer and Moderna's mRNA Covid vaccines have totaled more than $25 billion. The government paid Moderna $2.5 billion of taxpayer funds to develop the vaccine, and President Biden called on local leaders to use public money to bribe citizens to get the shots. The government fronted the costs of inventory, research, and advertising; the purchases were guaranteed; and there were widespread coercion efforts to have healthy people roll up their sleeves to get the shots.

These new glory days lack the "staggering liabilities" that formerly held private companies accountable. Citizens cannot sue vaccine manufacturers – including Pfizer, Moderna, and Johnson & Johnson – for any harms resulting from the Covid shots.

In February 2020, Secretary of Health and Human Services

Alex Azar invoked his powers under the Public Readiness and Emergency Preparedness (PREP) Act to provide liability immunity for medical companies in response to Covid. A Congressional report explains that this means that the corporations "cannot be sued for money damages in court" if they fall under the protection of Azar's orders.

In just 40 years, the system had been manipulated to serve corporations and disenfranchised citizens. Companies had once been responsible for the damages they caused, and their legal costs were an inherent risk in the free market system. Then, the NCVIA socialized that risk, passing the liabilities onto the taxpayer. Covid ushered in a third distinct stage: historic profits without any legal remedies for damages.

Americans bore the costs of producing the companies' products and purchasing the inventory of vaccines. In return, they faced mandates to take the shots and lost their right to hold commercial powers accountable. State, local, and federal governments required citizens to become customers for the country's richest companies at the same time they offered liability protection to the beneficiaries.

Predictably, pharmaceutical companies ignored warning signs from their clinical trials. In June 2023, confidential Pfizer documents revealed that the company observed over 1.5 million adverse reactions to Covid vaccines, including 75,000 vascular disorders, 100,000 blood and lymphatic disorders, 125,000 cardiac disorders, 175,000 reproductive disorders, and 190,000 respiratory disorders. Most of these occurred in healthy young adults, with 92% of reporters having zero comorbidities. In January 2025, Alex Berenson revealed that Moderna covered up the death of a preschool-aged child during its Covid mRNA vaccine trials. Despite federal requirements to report all trial information, the company withheld the truth of the child's death from "cardio-respiratory arrest" for years.

So how did that happen? In a healthy system, government officials would serve as vigilant regulators, remaining averse to corruption and deception. Instead, a revolving door emerged between the pharmaceutical industry and the government agencies responsible for monitoring them. This process subverted the purpose of the Seventh Amendment and created an unprecedented system of "glory days" for Big Pharma.

Subverting the Seventh Amendment

The Seventh Amendment guarantees the right to a jury trial in civil cases. At the time of its ratification in 1791, advocates of the amendment sought to protect the rights of common citizens against commercial powers that would otherwise corrupt the judicial system for their own benefit.

In *Federal Farmer IV* (1787), the author, writing under a pseudonym, argued that the jury system was "essential in every free country" to maintain the independence of the judiciary. Without the protection of the Seventh Amendment, the powerful – "the well born" – would wield the power of the judiciary, and they would be "generally disposed, and very naturally too, to favour those of their own description."

Sir William Blackstone called jury trials "the glory of the English law." Like *Federal Farmer IV*, he wrote that the absence of a jury would result in a judicial system run by men with "an involuntary bias towards those of their own rank and dignity." It became central to the cause of the Revolution when Jefferson listed King George III's denial of "the benefits of trial by jury" as a grievance in the Declaration of Independence.

Centuries later, we have returned to a system that denies citizens the right to jury trials. The judicial system has been warped for the benefit of commercial interests. The revolving door between Big Pharma and government, coupled with the denial of trial by jury, creates a system in which regulators favor "those of their own rank and dignity."

Congress enjoys a collusive and mutually beneficial relationship with the pharmaceutical industry. In 2018, Kaiser Health News found "Nearly 340 former congressional staffers now work for pharmaceutical companies or their lobbying firms."

The cozy relationship extends to unelected officials. Alex Azar, the HHS Secretary responsible for enacting the PREP Act, was president of the US division of Eli Lilly from 2012 to 2017. There, he oversaw significant price increases for drugs, including doubling the price of its insulin medicine. Scott Gottlieb resigned as Commissioner of the FDA in 2019 to join Pfizer's Board of Directors. During the pandemic, Gottlieb advocated for lockdowns and censorship, even encouraging Twitter to suppress pro-vaccine doctors who discussed natural immunity.

Biden White House Counselor Steve Richetti worked as a lobbyist for twenty years before joining the Biden Administration. His clients included Novartis, Eli Lilly, and Pfizer. The *New York Times* described him as "one of [Biden's] most loyal advisers, and someone Mr. Biden will almost certainly turn to in times of crisis or in stressful moments."

In May 2023, President Biden announced his nomination of Dr. Monica Bertagnolli as Director of the NIH. From 2015-2021, Bartagnolli received over $275 million in grants from Pfizer, amounting to 90% of her research funding.

The corruption is more direct than mere influence peddling. The pharmaceutical industry directly finances 75% of the FDA's drug division through "user fees," a negotiated rate paid to the agency during the drug approval process. "It's kind of like a devil's bargain," says Dr. Joseph Ross, a professor at Yale School of Medicine. "Because it turns…into the F.D.A. essentially asking industry, 'What can we do to secure this money?'" Senator Bernie Sanders put it more simply: "The industry, in a sense, is regulating itself."

The merger of power between the pharmaceutical industry and the U.S. government has created a system of mass profits without accountability. Just as Blackstone warned, this warped legal system allows the powerful to insulate those of their "own rank and dignity" from the accountability of jury trials.

Australian Senator Gerard Rennick explained: "Moderna, like Pfizer or Astra Zeneca (sic), aren't prepared to back up their 'safe and effective' mantra by underwriting the safety of the vaccines. They passed the buck onto governments whose politicians lacked the spine to stand up for the people they claim to represent."

In August 2023, Rennick questioned Moderna executives in the Australian Senate. "You're not prepared to underwrite the safety of your own vaccine," he explained. The Moderna executive repeatedly deflected, responding that "indemnities are a matter for policymakers."

But Big Pharma had deliberately inserted themselves in the policymaking process, usurping the role of the jury trial through the convergence of private and public power. Through billions of dollars in lobbying, Corona-law overtook the Western legal tradition and rigged the system to protect the most powerful forces in our society at the cost of the taxpayer, destroying the Seventh Amendment and its underlying purposes in the process.

The Influence Campaign: Lobbying, Advertising, and Deceiving

Pfizer and Big Pharma bolster this liability shield with widespread marketing campaigns and lobbying. From 2020 to 2022, the pharmaceutical and health products industry spent $1 billion on lobbying. For context, that was more than five times as much as the commercial banking industry spent on lobbying during the same time period. In those three years, Big Pharma spent more on lobbying than the oil, gas, alcohol, gambling, farming, and defense industries combined.

Big Pharma dedicates even more resources to buying the hearts and minds of the American people and their media outlets, expanding the influence campaign by controlling the information that consumers can access.

Pharmaceutical companies spent significantly more money on advertising and marketing than research and development (R&D) during Covid. In 2020, Pfizer spent $12 billion on sales and marketing and $9 billion on R&D. That year, Johnson & Johnson devoted $22 billion to sales and marketing and $12 billion to R&D.

Combined, AbbVie, Pfizer, Novartis, GlaxoSmithKline, Sanofi, Bayer, and J&J spent 50% more on advertising than R&D in 2020. They advertise prescription products that consumers cannot get on their own, indicating that the spending is designed to control the news media, not increase drug sales.

"The key point about pharma advertising is they don't spend to impact customers who watch news. It's to impact the news itself," explains former pharmaceutical consultant Calley Means. "Pharma sees ad spending as part of their lobbying and public affairs budget. It is a way to buy off news networks to influence the debate."

Just as Means described, billions of dollars in advertising resulted in millions of Americans tuning into programming sponsored by Pfizer, including *Good Morning America*, *CBS This Morning*, *Meet the Press*, *60 Minutes*, *CNN Tonight*, *Erin Burnett OutFront*, *This Week with George Stephanopoulos*, *Anderson Cooper 360*, and *ABC Nightline*. For the most part, reporters obsequiously bowed to the thinly veiled system of paying off the Fourth Estate. Throughout Covid, the press promoted Big Pharma's products and seldom mentioned its history of unjust enrichment, fraud, and criminal pleas

This media landscape subjected Americans to the approved lies of the corporate press. Talking heads and government officials worked in unison to support their financial sponsors through moral bludgeoning.

"Literally the only people dying are the unvaccinated," Chuck Todd told his viewers. "And for those of you spreading misinformation, shame on you. Shame on you. I don't know how some of you sleep at night." By 2022, the majority of people dying from Covid were vaccinated.

Mika Brzezinski took a similarly direct approach to her MSNBC viewers: "You are the unvaccinated, you are the problem." The White House, dedicated viewers of *Morning Joe*, adopted Mika's strident tone. "We've been patient, but our patience is wearing thin," President Biden told the unvaccinated in September in 2021. "And your refusal has cost all of us."

CNN's Don Lemon told Chris Cuomo, "the only people you can blame – this isn't shaming, this is the truth…maybe they should be shamed – are the unvaccinated." MSNBC's Jonathan Capehart lectured the unvaccinated, "Anyone you come into contact with will blame you. As will the rest of us, who have done the right thing by getting vaccinated."

"There is no excuse — no excuse for anyone being unvaccinated," Biden scolded his citizens in 2022.

Frequent CNN contributor Dr. Leana Wen repeatedly expressed her outrage at the unvaccinated. "People are not behaving honorably. The unvaccinated are basically saying, Well it's open season for me." She told viewers that choosing to stay unvaccinated was akin to "the choice to drive intoxicated."

In the *Los Angeles Times*, columnist Michael Hiltzik delivered the headline: "Mocking anti-vaxxers' COVID deaths is ghoulish, yes — but may be necessary."

Howard Stern called for mandatory vaccinations and told those who disagreed with him, "Fuck your freedom." But Stern was no longer a gadfly provocateur; he was a mouthpiece for the most powerful entities in the country, who welcomed the opportunity to tarnish the Bill of Rights in a liability-free nation of mandates.

Unavoidably Unsafe, Undeniably Ineffective, and Unapologetically Corrupt

The Biden White House bolstered the private-sector influence campaign, with the federal government shelling out billions to media companies to advertise the Covid vaccines. In March 2022, *Blaze* reported:

"In response to a FOIA request filed by TheBlaze, HHS revealed that it purchased advertising from major news networks including ABC, CBS, and NBC, as well as cable TV news stations Fox News, CNN, and MSNBC, legacy media publications including the New York Post, the Los Angeles Times, and the Washington Post, digital media companies like BuzzFeed News and Newsmax, and hundreds of local newspapers and TV stations. These outlets were collectively responsible for publishing countless articles and video segments regarding the vaccine that were nearly uniformly positive about the vaccine in terms of both its efficacy and safety."

"Safe and effective" became echoed so frequently in the media landscape that few bothered to investigate whether the tagline was true. The slogan contradicted long-standing understandings of inherent risk. In 1986, the House Energy and Commerce Committee issued a report that described vaccines as "unavoidably unsafe." The Supreme Court cited the "unavoidably unsafe" determination, describing the products "in the present state of human knowledge," as "quite incapable of being made safe for their intended and ordinary use."

Further, there was never evidence that the shots were "effective." A Pfizer study showed that 20% of those who received the company's Covid vaccines got Covid within two months, While 1% of the participants in the trial reported "cardiac disorders" after their first shots. Company executives admitted under sworn testimony that the company never tested the efficacy of the vaccines against transmission before marketing them.

In October 2022, Pfizer spokeswoman Janine Small appeared at a European Parliament hearing. "Was the Pfizer Covid vaccine tested on stopping transmission of the virus before it entered the market?" asked Dutch MEP Rob Roos. "No!" Small responded emphatically. "We had to really move at the speed of science to really understand what is taking place in the market; and from that point of view, we had to do everything at risk."

The "risk" appeared to be substantial. Days before Small's testimony, Florida Surgeon General Joseph Ladapo released an analysis showing an 84% increase in the relative incidence of cardiac-related death in males 18-39 within 28 days of mRNA vaccination.

By June 2021, the United States Vaccine Adverse Effective Reporting System (VAERS) reported 4,812 deaths from the Covid vaccine as well as 21,440 hospitalizations. For context, VAERS has reported just 5,039 deaths from all other vaccine reports combined since 1990. In January 2023, VAERS exceeded one million adverse events reported from the Covid vaccine as well as 21,000 deaths, with 30% of those deaths taking place within 48 hours of vaccination. The European Medicines Agency linked Covid vaccines to facial paralysis, tingling sensations, numbness, and tinnitus. The CDC later admitted that the shots are linked to heart inflammation (myocarditis), particularly in young men, as well as Guillain-Barre syndrome, and blood clotting.

Dr. Buddy Creech, 50, led Covid vaccine trials at Vanderbilt University before developing tinnitus and heart racing after receiving the shot. Creech said his tinnitus and racing heart lasted about a week after each shot. "When our patients experience a side effect that may or may not be related to the vaccine, we owe it to them to investigate that as completely as we can," he told the *New York Times*.

"Safe and effective" turned out to be a pharmaceutical advertising slogan parroted in the press corps that relied on the steady stream of advertising revenue from the companies it was covering. The US government also joined the coverup in its fanatical crusade to jab as many citizens as possible.

In January 2024, *the Epoch Times* revealed that the CDC drafted an "alert on myocarditis and mRNA vaccines" in May 2021 for state and local officials warning them of the connection between heart inflammation and Covid-19 shots. The author of the report, Dr. Demetre Daskalakis, evidently decided not to publicize his findings.

The CDC later sent repeated alerts encouraging Covid-19 vaccination but never published its warnings on myocarditis. Dr. Tracy Hoeg, a California epidemiologist, told the *Epoch Times*, "We had data from our own Department of Defense at this time indicating it was a real safety signal and two fatal post-Pfizer vaccination myocarditis cases had already been reported in Israel."

When Daskalakis drafted the alert, the overwhelming majority of American teenagers had not received Covid shots. No state had a vaccination rate above 14% for 12- to 17-year-olds. In California, 90% of that age cohort was unvaccinated. In the following two years, the CDC never published its alert, and the country injected millions of teenagers with the shots. Within two years, 84% of California teenagers had at least one dose of a Covid vaccine; more than one in five had received a booster.

Big Pharma's influence campaign extended beyond the media landscape. Medical journals have long been beholden to corporate interests. As of 2017, half of the editors of American medical journals receive payments from drug companies. Companies pay doctors to list themselves as the authors to enhance their reports' credibility in a system known as "medical ghost-writing."

Once Covid vaccines came along, Pfizer paid organizations to promote vaccine mandates for employees. In August 2021, Chicago Urban League President Karen Freeman-Wilson announced the organization's support for Covid vaccine mandates. She did not disclose that her group had just received a $100,000 grant from Pfizer to launch a "vaccine safety and effectiveness campaign." Weeks later, the National Consumers League announced, "it has become evidence that employer mandates are effective at nudging reluctant people to get the Covid-19 vaccine." The previous month, Pfizer gave the group $75,000 for "vaccine policy efforts." The

American Academy of Pediatrics had local chapters lobby for pro-vaccine state policies after receiving $250,000 from Pfizer, including "immunization legislation" advocacy grants.

Other groups that promoted mandates after receiving Pfizer grants included the National Consumers League, the American Pharmacists Association, the American College of Preventive Medicine, the American Society for Clinical Pathology, and the American College of Emergency Physicians. None of them disclosed their financial incentives.

There was an integrated public relations strategy for pharmaceutical companies to maintain their protected status of supra-legal profiteers. Not only did they purchase the obedience of the news media, but they also used financial coercion to ensure that the medical establishment had no power to oppose them.

Upon the release of Pfizer's 2022 Annual Report, CEO Albert Bourla stressed the importance of customer's "positive perception" of the pharmaceutical giant.

"2022 was a record-breaking year for Pfizer, not only in terms of revenue and earnings per share, which were the highest in our long history," Bourla noted. "But more importantly, in terms of the percentage of patients who have a positive perception of Pfizer and the work we do."

The industry dedicated billions of dollars to manipulating Americans into taking its products while their government stripped them of their right to legal action; citizens, devoid of the ability to hold the companies accountable in the court of law, continue to subsidize the federal-pharmaceutical hegemon with their tax dollars.

In effect, the federal government sold the Seventh Amendment to the largest lobbying force in the country. This transferred power from the citizenry to the nation's ruling class and exchanged a constitutional right for a corporate liability shield.

THE ROLE OF THE MILITARY

The year 2020 introduced a barrage of previously obscure phrases to the forefront of the American lexicon. *Social distancing, PCR tests, misinformation, mRNA platforms, remote learning, Zoom school, lockdowns, super-spreader, net zero, Juneteenth, epidemiologists, BIPOC,* and so on. In the onslaught of new terms and cultural norms, Americans lost sight of a simple question: who was in charge?

There were debates about the influence of Fauci and the tension between state and federal initiatives. Right- and left-wing media distracted the citizenry with sensational headlines about proles killing grandmas, celebrities singing John Lennon, and nurses choreographing dance routines. Amid the manic news cycles, nobody seemed to know who was responsible for the mass mobilization of government resources.

At its core, the Covid response was a military operation. It uncovered the entangled webs of ostensibly distinct structures of military and health operations. The National Security Council sparked the panicked response, the Department of Homeland Security oversaw lockdowns, the Intelligence Community, led by the CIA, censored dissent, and the Department of Defense administered the vaccine push.

Contingency plans involved martial law, not nationalization of hospitals. The first White House official to advocate for overturning American society was not Anthony Fauci; it was Deputy National Security Advisor Matthew Pottinger. Taken as a whole, the military apparatus overthrew the civilian government. It was a bloodless coup.

The CIA's Role From the Outset

In January 2025, journalist Seymour Hersh revealed that a CIA spy worked at the Wuhan Institute of Virology through 2019 and 2020. According to Hersh, "The asset, highly regarded within the CIA, was recruited while in graduate school in the United States." In 2019, the spy warned that "China was doing both offensive and defensive work" with pathogens, and that there had been a laboratory accident that resulted in the infection of a researcher.

As Dr. Fauci led the movement to publish the "proximal origin" paper, he also used the power of America's clandestine services to silence potential critics. Fauci began taking secret meetings at CIA headquarters "without a record of entry" in order to "influence its Covid-19 origins investigation," according to a whistleblower (though Fauci has denied those claims). "He knew what was going on...He was covering his ass and he was trying to do it with the Intel community," the whistleblower told Congress. "He came multiple times and he was treated like a rock star by the Weapons and Counter Proliferation Mission Center."

Fauci had long bridged the worlds of public health and American spycraft. After the terrorist and Anthrax attacks of 2001, the United States became preoccupied with biosecurity to protect against bioweapons, pandemics, and chemical attacks. At

Fort Detrick, Maryland, which historian Stephen Kinzer describes as "the Army's principal base for biological research," the spy world developed "the nerve center of the CIA's hidden chemical and mind control empire."

The FBI later determined that the 2001 Anthrax attacks came from a lone, disgruntled Fort Detrick scientist named Bruce Ivins (though law enforcement did not charge him until after he committed suicide in 2008). That theory has faced intense scrutiny from figures across the political landscape, including Christopher Ketcham, Glenn Greenwald, and the National Academy of Sciences. But all agreed that the Anthrax came from inside the United States Intelligence Community.

Francis Boyle, a professor of law at the University of Illinois who drafted the 1989 Biological Weapons Anti-Terrorism Act signed by President George H.W. Bush, argued that a full review of the evidence from the 2001 Anthrax attacks would have "led directly back to a secret but officially sponsored US government biowarfare program that was illegal and criminal," specifically citing potential involvement from the Pentagon, the CIA, and public-private partnerships.

Rather than reform, however, Congress chose to grow the bioweapons machinery. Following 9/11 and the PATRIOT Act, Fauci received a 68-percent pay increase (making him the highest paid federal employee in the country) to "appropriately compensate him for the level of responsibility...especially as it relates to his work on biodefense research activities." In 2002, he spearheaded a multi-billion expansion of Fort Detrick.

Meanwhile, Fauci and the US Government continued to funnel money to foreign groups pursuing gain-of-function research, such as the Wuhan Institute of Virology, where it is now known that the Intelligence Community implanted spies.

Until 2020, the concept of a clandestine, supra-national bioweapons program would have sounded far-fetched to even conspiratorial minds. But the emergence of Covid threatened to unveil the illicit programs run by spymasters and the public health apparatus. In a desperate attempt to evade accountability, the Intelligence Community joined the cover-up of the lab leak.

The CIA offered bribes to scientists to bury findings refuting the "proximal origin" thesis led by Fauci, Farrar, Andersen, and Holmes, according to a whistleblower. The House Oversight Committee explained: "According to the whistleblower, at the end of its review, six of the seven members of the Team believed the intelligence and science were sufficient to make a low confidence assessment that COVID-19 originated from a laboratory in Wuhan, China." Then, however, the whistleblower reported that the "six members were given a significant monetary incentive to change their position."

Meanwhile, scientists in the Department of Defense compiled significant evidence that suggested a lab leak. Like others, they analyzed the "furin cleavage" site and evidence stemming from the Wuhan Institute of Virology. But when they went to deliver their findings to the White House, President Biden's Director of National Intelligence, Avril Haines, banned them from presenting their evidence or participating in a discussion on the origins of the virus.

In January 2025, following President Trump's second inauguration, John Ratcliffe, the recently installed head of the CIA, announced that the agency believed that a lab leak was the most likely source of Covid. "I think our intelligence, our science and our common sense all really dictate that the origin of Covid was a leak at the Wuhan Institute of Virology," Ratcliffe told Breitbart News.

As outlined in "The First Amendment Versus the U.S. Security State," the Intelligence Community was integral to the nation's censorship crusade. CISA, an agency within the Department of Homeland Security, was responsible for dividing the workforce into labels of "essential" and "nonessential" during lockdowns and then implemented a program known as "switchboarding," where CISA officials dictated to Big Tech platforms what content was permissible or prohibited speech. Their contempt for free speech was indisputable. CISA Director Jen Easterly testified in *Missouri v. Biden*, "I think [it] is really, really dangerous if people get to pick their own facts."

Unrelenting, the Department of Homeland Security announced in April 2022 that it would establish a "Disinformation Governance Board," which was to be headed by Democratic activist Nina Jankowicz. According to *Politico*, Biden's Ministry of Truth was charged with "countering misinformation." The Ministry of Truth was only discontinued when the absurdity of its chief censor, Jankowicz, caused sufficient blowback from the public.

Further, the Intelligence Community's influence extended to the highest levels of the White House. Beginning in January 2020, there was an insidious usurpation of the chain of command, and the civilian government was overtaken by a rogue band of military officials. That coup reached the National Security Council through a little-known official named Matthew Pottinger.

Matthew Pottinger and the National Security Council

Matthew Pottinger began his career as a journalist for the *Wall Street Journal* before enlisting in the Marines in 2005. He worked a series of assignments in Asia and later reflected, "Living in China shows you what a nondemocratic country can do to its citizens."

In 2017, he joined the Trump Administration as deputy national security advisor, and Politico described him as "the National Security Council's top Asia hand."

In 2020, as deputy national security advisor, he helped usher in a military junta that showed Americans *what a nondemocratic country can do to its citizens*. On January 14, Pottinger breached protocol by unilaterally calling the first interagency meeting on the coronavirus. On January 27, he again summoned officials in the White House Situation Room to address the coronavirus. While others called for measured responses, Pottinger advocated for travel bans and lockdowns.

In *Nightmare Scenario*, *Washington Post* reporter Yasmeen Abutaleb writes:

> "Few people in the room knew it, but Pottinger had actually called the meeting. The Chinese weren't providing the US government much information about the virus, and Pottinger didn't trust what they were disclosing anyway. He had spent two weeks scouring Chinese social media feeds and had uncovered dramatic reports of the new infectious disease suggesting that it was much worse than the Chinese government had revealed. He had also seen reports that the virus might have escaped from a lab in Wuhan, China. There were too many unanswered questions. He told everyone in the Sit Room that they needed to consider enacting a travel ban immediately: ban all travel from China; shut it down...[Pottinger] said that dramatic actions would need to be taken."

The following day, Pottinger instructed his wife to text her friend Deborah Birx to meet him in the West Wing. "Matt got to the point quickly," Birx wrote in her memoir. "He offered me the position of White House spokesperson on the virus."

Three days later, Pottinger suggested lockdowns on the American public. He raised concerns of asymptomatic spread after reading Chinese social media sources. From the outset, he suspected the virus was the result of a laboratory leak, though his colleagues in the Intelligence Community publicly denigrated that thesis as "conspiratorial." When health experts responded that there was no history of coronaviruses spreading through asymptomatic carriers, Pottinger increased his calls for drastic measures. Without any scientific basis, Pottinger advocated for universal masking, saying the policy had no "downside."

According to Abutaleb, Pottinger asked, "What was the downside in having people cover their faces while they waited for more data and research about how effective masks might be?"

In "The Talented Mr. Pottinger," attorney Michael Senger details the enormous control Pottinger had over the early response to the coronavirus, especially with respect to masking, travel bans, lockdowns, and hysteria surrounding "asymptomatic spread" of the virus.

While media sources and government officials berated critics to "trust the experts," the leading proponent of lockdowns in the White House was a military alarmist with no understanding of epidemiology and a disregard for the chain of command. He was perhaps the most influential spreader of disinformation from the onset of the pandemic.

Senger summarizes Pottinger's influence on the American response to Covid as a "singularly outsized role:"

"Pottinger may have simply been overly-trusting of his sources, thinking they were the little people in China trying to help their American friends. But why did Pottinger push

so hard for sweeping Chinese policies like mask mandates
that were far outside his field of expertise? Why did he
so often breach protocol? Why seek out and appoint
Deborah Birx?"

Beyond his influence within the White House, Pottinger and
similar actors sowed panic over the novel coronavirus through the
media. On March 7, 2020, Tucker Carlson drove to Mar-a-Lago
to warn Trump of the disastrous effects of Covid, information
he received from a "nonpolitical person with access to a lot of
intelligence."

Ten days later, Carlson explained his trip to Palm Beach to
Vanity Fair:

> "Well, in January is when we first started covering it on
> the show...And then I happened to be speaking a couple of
> days later to someone who works in the US government,
> a nonpolitical person with access to a lot of intelligence.
> He said the Chinese are lying about the extent of this.
> They won't let international health inspectors in. They're
> blocking WHO and this could infect millions of people, a
> high percentage of them. And this was a highly informed
> person, very informed, and again, a nonpolitical person
> with no reason to lie about it in either direction. So that
> really got my attention."

During his trip to Mar-a-Lago, Carlson warned President
Trump that he could lose the election over Covid and that sources
with connections in China insisted that the virus was far more
devastating than had been previously reported. Carlson's source
matches an exact description of Pottinger. He was a nonpolitical

member of the Trump Administration with bipartisan support and access to the highest levels of intelligence. He had extensive experience in China and was adamant that the coronavirus would devastate society.

Jeffrey Tucker writes: "we should not underestimate the importance of this turn of events and the likely role of Pottinger in convincing Tucker of the case for tremendous alarm and panic. Without that, Trump might not have caved and the base would have rallied around him."

And just before that alarm reached the public, the Intelligence Community and its liaisons positioned themselves to triumph amidst the forthcoming chaos.

In February 2020, Senator Richard Burr (R-NC) was the Chair of the Senate Intelligence Committee, one of the most powerful and sought-after positions in Washington. His perch gave him access to information that remained classified to nearly all of his Senate colleagues. On February 13, 2020, as Burr received intelligence on the coronavirus (a full month ahead of lockdowns), he placed a 50-second phone call to his brother-in-law, Gerald Fauth. Within minutes, Fauth called his stockbroker to begin liquidating his portfolio. Meanwhile, Senator Burr delivered public assurances that the country was "better prepared than ever before to face emerging public-health threats." Behind closed doors, however, Burr prepared for economic and national disaster. After receiving nonpublic briefings on the emergence of the virus and the nation's planned response, Senator Burr sold $1.6 million of stock from his retirement portfolio.

Around the same time, Senator Kelly Loeffler (R-GA) and her husband sold $20 million in stocks after attending a confidential briefing on the coronavirus. At the same time, they purchased stocks, including health care equities, that proved very successful in the coming months.

On February 20, 2020, the worldwide economic downturn began. On March 10, the Dow suffered what was then its fourth-worst day ever, with the market losing nearly 10% of its value. That crash was outdone a week later on March 16 when the Dow suffered its third-worst day ever and the Dow Jones Industrial Average crashed 12.9%. In April, the price of crude oil turned negative (meaning producers had to pay buyers to take barrels) for the first time in American history.

And so an illicit cycle of activities began at the behest of the Intelligence Community. Those with access to the levers of power sought to profit or advance their careers, and their incentive was to induce alarm and subservience from the citizenry.

It is now clear that a cabal, led by the National Security Council, violated the chain of command, misled the media, panicked the American public, and developed response plans before any elected official went through the channels of due process. It prompted the largest violation of civil liberties in American history, and it is traceable to the highest levels of the nation's military. That junta then overtook the Covid response and the American government without anyone seeming to take notice.

The Military Takes Over the Covid Response

Weeks before the first stay-at-home order, the military ordered standby orders "to prepare for the possibility of some form of martial law," *Newsweek* reported. In February 2020, three contingency operations called upon the military to administer government operations by circumventing the US Constitution. Military commanders would be placed across the United States, and General Terrence J. O'Shaughnessy would lead the country as "combatant commander." Dictator O'Shaughnessy never came to power, but the military community took charge of the Covid response behind the scenes.

Beginning in March 2020, the National Security Council and the Department of Homeland Security replaced the Department of Health and Human Services as the lead actors in the domestic efforts against Covid.

Their roles were not ceremonial; the military agencies were inseparably tied to the leading public health bureaucrats. Pottinger and the NSC were responsible for appointing Deborah Birx to the Covid response team. "We brought into the White House Debi Birx," explained Trump's National Security Advisor on March 11, 2020.

Without any announcement, the country's leading military officials overtook the most widespread suppression of civil liberties in American history.

Government documents from March 13, 2020, showed that the National Security Council had taken control of the nation's Covid policy. Five days later, President Trump invoked the Stafford Act, which made FEMA, a branch of the Department of Homeland Security, the "Lead Federal Agency" (LFA) in the pandemic response, replacing the Department of Health and Human Services. From then on, HHS (including the CDC, NIAID, and the NIH) had no official leadership role in the response to Covid.

The week that the military replaced the health apparatus as the leaders of the Covid response coincided with the beginning of lockdowns on March 16. Representative government had ceased to exist in the United States. Americans had never heard of Robert O'Brien or Matthew Pottinger, but they were responsible for implanting the largest mobilization of government resources in world history. With hindsight, it was a clear and deliberate military operation.

The United States, meanwhile, had completed the construction of the first federal quarantine camp in over a century in January 2020, which the *New York Times* described as "just in time to receive 15 American passengers from the coronavirus-infested Diamond Princess cruise ship." The Pentagon later announced that it would expand the facility, located in Omaha, Nebraska, in coordination with a slew of other federal entities, including the Department of Homeland Security.

In July 2020, the CDC published plans for nationwide quarantine camps, in which the US Government, led by the armed services, would forcibly isolate patients, ban them from social contacts, and strip them of all physical access to the outside world other than the delivery of food and cleaning supplies. "The implementation of this approach will involve careful planning, additional resources, strict adherence and strong multi-sector coordination," the CDC explained.

Underpinning this plan was the strength of the US military, which was charged with carrying out the Covid response. Thus, the existing government used the military to quietly restructure society, abolishing its constitution and its longest-standing freedoms. The results were tyrannical, nonsensical, and devastating. Soon thereafter, the military led the next crusade in the Covid coup.

The Department of Defense and Vaccines

In 1958, the US Department of Defense established the Defense Advanced Research Projects Agency (DARPA) to promote research and development of military-level technology following the Soviet Union's launch of Sputnik the previous year. In the ensuing decades, DARPA devised technology that laid the foundation for the internet, GPS, Agent Orange, and mRNA gene therapy.

In *Imagineers of War: The Untold Story of DARPA*, Sharon

Weinberger writes that DARPA's "allure of applying the wizardry of science and technology to warfare" has made wars "more inviting" and "entangled the United States in a 'forever war.'"

Following the 2001 terrorist and anthrax attacks, the Department of Defense began investing tens of billions of dollars into vaccines and medical initiatives. The *Lancet* explains:

"Total US biodefense funding dramatically increased from ~$700,000,000 in 2001 to ~$4,000,000,000 spent in 2002; the peak of funding in 2005 was worth nearly $8,000,000,000 and continued with steady average spending around $5,000,000,000."

In 2003, Dr. Anthony Fauci articulated his biodefense vision: "...the goal within the next 20 years is to have 'bug to drug' within 24 hours. This would meet the challenge of genetically engineered bioagents."

The 9/11 response also paved the way for "emergency use authorization," a designation from the US Food and Drug Administration (FDA) that allows unapproved medical products to be used during a public health emergency. Harvard Law's Bill of Health explains, "Ultimately, it was the War on Terror that would give rise to emergency use authorization."

In the ensuing 20 years, the United States invested over $100 billion in the biodefense industry, including programs called "ADEPT" and the "Pandemic Preparedness Platform," which provided the capital for the initial development of mRNA technology. In 2013, DARPA provided the initial investment in Moderna.

In September 2019, President Trump signed an Executive Order on "Modernizing Influenza Vaccines," which directed government agencies, including the Department of Defense to develop a "5-year national plan to promote the use of more agile and scalable vaccine manufacturing technologies." Six months later, the pandemic response took center stage, and the Pentagon prepared to weaponize its biodefense infrastructure.

Later that year, the US Government entered into a vaccine manufacturing agreement with Pfizer and BioNTech. By July, the agreement encompassed a minimum of 100 million doses of a "vaccine to prevent COVID-19" and a payment of at least $1.95 billion. The agreement also allowed for future procurement of hundreds of millions of additional doses. Investigative journalist Debbie Lerman writes: "That's a lot of money for a lot of items, especially since the vaccines had not yet been tested, approved, or manufactured to scale and, as the agreement stated, were purely 'aspirational.'"

In the following months, "Operation Warp Speed" only increased the role of the military in an initiative that ostensibly came from the private sector. In November 2020, the *New York Times* described how "the role of the military has been less public and more pervasive" in the Covid vaccine response than Americans realized. The article recounted how the Defense Department acquired facilities, raw materials, permits, and medical supplies for the vaccine manufacturers and orchestrated supply chain management, distribution initiatives, and "every logistical detail you could think of."

Pentagon planners considered every potential disruption to the project, but the government deliberately hid the involvement of the military from the public. "Concerns about conspiracy theories surrounding the vaccines are even more reason to keep the military out of sight," the *Times* explained. The Chief Operating Officer of Operation Warp Speed, Four Star General Gustave F. Perna, had to manage disgruntled public health officials who complained "that the military's role in Operation Warp Speed was too large," according to the *Times*.

But the Defense Department's influence was not limited to procurement or logistics; it was central to the approval and dissemination of the shots. The Harvard Law Bill of Health explains that for emergency use authorizations, "[t]he record indicates that Congress was focused on the threat of bioterror specifically, not on preparing for a naturally-occurring pandemic."

Debbie Lerman writes: "Here's the kicker about EUA: because it was intended to be issued only in war and WMD-related emergencies, there are no legal requirements for how it is issued, beyond the determination of the FDA that such authorization is appropriate. No legal standards for how clinical trials are conducted. No laws regulating the manufacturing processes. Only 'reasonable beliefs' based on whatever evidence is available to the FDA at the time that it makes its determination."

Thus, the Department of Defense used the infrastructure of emergency war powers stemming from the PATRIOT Act to evade traditional testing and safety protocol. Once Secretary of Health and Human Services Secretary Alex Azar invoked the PREP Act, the Department of Defense and the FDA were able to begin vaccine rollouts under emergency use authorization.

This had critical downstream effects. Notably, the FDA did not require any safety efficacy data from clinical trials to authorize the EUA, and any clinical trials related to the EUA process were not required to comply with any regulatory standards. Coupled with the nearly all-encompassing immunity granted to vaccine manufacturers, every incentive encouraged rushing a flawed shot to the market.

By June 2021, the United States Vaccine Adverse Effective

Reporting System (VAERS) reported 4,812 deaths from the Covid vaccine as well as 21,440 hospitalizations. In January 2023, VAERS exceeded one million adverse events reported from the Covid vaccine as well as 21,000 deaths (four times as many deaths as VAERS has recorded from all other vaccine reports combined since 1990), with 30% of those deaths taking place within 48 hours of vaccination. In the following years, regulatory agencies and studies belatedly acknowledged vaccine injuries, including blood-clotting, myocarditis, reduced sperm count, Guillain-Barre syndrome, facial paralysis, tinnitus, and death.

American citizens felt it from the beginning; some sense that normal law was no longer in operation. The whole of society, in many countries, was experiencing something closer to martial law. There were only orders, not legislation. The orders were often cast as recommendations but enforced as mandates. The lines of authority were scrambled and confusion reigned throughout, with fear replacing rational judgment.

It was always unclear precisely who was in charge, and that became more apparent when the President himself started posting wishes for a return to normalcy on his social media accounts. Was he not in charge? In many ways, no; the military was running the show from behind the scenes, using public health agencies as cover.

Of all features of the Covid response, this is the one that remains least explained, least explored, and least understood. That is because vast amounts of the documentation, from the lockdowns to the countermeasures called vaccines, still remain cloaked under the cover of being classified.

AFTER THE COVID DEBACLE

In March 1913, a man on horseback galloped into downtown Columbus, Ohio shouting, "The dam has burst!" Men ran into the streets. "Go east," they yelled. "Go east," away from the impending flood.

The panic was contagious. The first group began to run, and others soon followed. Shop owners and pedestrians joined the dash. Dozens turned to scores, scores to hundreds, multiplying until 2,000 Ohioans ran eastward.

"Like a flash, business on High street was paralyzed, the whole city was thrown into a panic, rescue work in the flood district was hurriedly abandoned, the river's east brink from a mile was cleared of humanity," the *Columbus Citizen* reported. "Never before in the history of Columbus was there such a scene of panic, even consternation. Through alleys, down street, down stairways, out of windows, people hurried, tumbled, ran, shouted and fairly fought each other in their almost mad rush."

The panic blinded the stampede to its surroundings. The sun was shining, and their ankles remained dry. The thrill was all-consuming. They ran shoulder-to-shoulder with their neighbors for six miles. Some ran twice as far as they jockeyed for high ground.

"In a twinkling the streets became a tangled jam of men and women, who had abandoned desk and counter to seek places of safety," the *Ohio State Journal* wrote. They flouted all traditional concerns. Housewives sprinted outside while stoves burned; shopkeepers joined the mob with doors unlocked; men sprinted past the less agile without offering to help. Horses ran out from their stables and through the streets, "adding confusion to the eddying torrent of people and vehicles," the paper reported.

"A visitor in an airplane, looking down on the straggling, agitated masses of people below, would have been hard put to it to divine a reason for the phenomenon," wrote James Thurber, who was in Columbus that day. "It must have inspired, in such an observer, a peculiar kind of terror."

As legs began to tire, the sprint turned to a jog, then a trot, then a walk, then a rest. The news spread that the dam had not broken at all. The residents returned to Columbus to find the flood had never arrived.

"The next day, the city went about its business as if nothing had happened, but there was no joking," Thurber wrote. One reporter later admitted, "There was a silent agreement among us on the paper that the panic run was best forgotten." Discussing the madness would be an admission of their mammalian shortcomings, an acknowledgement of how their instinct to follow an irrational crowd blinded them to obvious truths.

Now, the world finds itself in a similar position with respect to Coronamania, though the damage is far more profound. To various degrees, all were complicit. Some ran full speed with the crowds, others remained silent as the pathology spread. Only a few are curious about who was pushing the controls behind the scenes, how they managed to break through all restrictions on such schemes, the trillions doled out to business interests, and how these huge attacks on all civilized precepts of social and economic functioning swept the world.

Many took months or years to recognize that false premises had underpinned the government response that overturned their way of life. Those who resisted wish they had done so earlier. Those at the forefront wish they had been more vocal and effective.

Agitated masses of people abandoned their daily routines based on the error-ridden declarations of those in authority. Americans injected themselves with experimental shots and kept their children out of school. They castigated their neighbors and instituted systems of medical apartheid in cities and campuses. They shut down the kids' schools, covered their faces, and taught the children that people are nothing but disease vectors.

The orthodox worshipers of Government edicts banned religious gatherings, insisted the elderly die alone, and offered indulgences for their political allies. Reprehensibly, the organs of power, intertwined in a conspiracy of shared interests, promoted the panic and exploited the destruction they sowed.

Homicides, childhood suicides, and mental illness skyrocketed while lockdowns gutted the middle class. The Federal Reserve printed three hundred years' worth of spending in two months, and fraudsters stole at least tens of billions from Covid relief programs. The federal deficit more than tripled, and studies suggest the pandemic response will cost Americans $16 trillion over the next decade.

Corporate interests looted the public treasury. Mayors criminalized Easter worship, and bureaucrats used GPS data to monitor church attendance. Millions of unvetted men from the third world poured into our country while unvaccinated Americans died after being denied organ transplants.

Supposed monetary experts flooded the economy with trillions in liquidity while keeping interest rates near zero. The military fired healthy men for refusing to take ineffective shots. Government policies transferred $4 trillion from the middle class to tech oligarchs and permanently closed businesses across the country.

The powerful heeded Rahm Emanuel's advice and capitalized on the crisis. The Constitution was designed to restrain the powerful, but public health became the pretext to unshackle aspiring tyrants from its limitations. The Intelligence Community, through bribes, deception, and coercion, overturned the republic. Government and private industry merged forces to unleash remarkable tyranny and unprecedented wealth accumulation.

In March 2025, Dr. Scott Atlas, the White House's chief voice of dissent protesting Coronamania in 2020, reflected: "The mismanagement of the pandemic hit us personally and exposed a massive, across-the-board institutional failure. It was the most tragic breakdown of leadership and ethics that free societies have seen in our lifetimes."

After ten weeks of lockdowns, the regime revealed its true aims. *Fifteen days to flatten the curve* was merely the "first step leading to longer and more aggressive interventions," as Birx admitted in her memoir.

Their aspirations were far more grandiose. As Dr. Fauci later wrote in *Cell*, they were prepared to "rebuild the infrastructures of human existence." Then, a Minnesota police officer put his knee on the neck of George Floyd, a career criminal with heart disease, a Covid infection, and enough fentanyl and methamphetamine in his system to classify as an overdose.

With Floyd's death, the pretext of "public health" disappeared, and *social justice* catalyzed their mission to "rebuild the infrastructure of human existence." School curricula, social media content policies, investment criteria, corporate hierarchies, Supreme Court nominations, Vice President selections, and every aspect of American life became dominated by a pernicious new ideology under the innocuous banner of inclusivity.

Meritocracy, tradition, and equality were quickly supplanted by diversity, equity, and inclusion. Those new buzzwords were merely covers for the ideology of nihilism and iconoclasm they mandated.

As the liberties enshrined in the Bill of Rights disappeared from daily life, so too did the physical connections to the American past. The statues came tumbling down, and shared language became taboo. While the churches remained shuttered, radicals preached a creed of anti-white, anti-Western vitriol. Freedom became reserved for those who subscribed to the new and amorphous creed. The nation added trillions to its deficit and destroyed institutions that took generations to build.

When the panic swept over the public and its representatives, the Supreme Court remained derelict, greenlighting the steamrolling of civil liberties. The Bill of Rights proved to be no more than "parchment guarantees." As Justice Antonin Scalia explained, these enumerated rights — habeas corpus, freedom of speech, free exercise of religion, freedom of movement, the right to jury trials, equality under the law – were "not worth the paper they were printed on."

The Framers designed a structure of government and the accompanying separation of powers to protect those liberties. Federalism intended for states to resist national tyranny; a bicameral legislature created systems meant to combat radicalism; separating the power of "the purse and the sword" – of spending and of executive power – was intended to limit despotism; judicial review would protect individual rights against the fervor of the mob; separate spheres of public and private entities would create an antagonistic balance between the rule of law and innovation.

But in the Covid response, a cabal, led by forces in the Intelligence Community and the US Military, abolished those safeguards. The federal government worked to punish insubordinate states. The legislature and the Federal Reserve opened the public coffers for the country's most powerful forces to loot at will. The Supreme Court abandoned its role as a protector of liberty as the Chief Justice conjured a pandemic exception to jurisprudence. Unmitigated hysteria opened the opportunity for a *coup d'etat* as the regime marched in lockstep toward tyranny.

Five years later, fundamental questions remain unanswered, and threats are unabated. The origins of the pandemic remain clouded in confidentiality and mystery.

There has been no effort to curb the extra-constitutional excesses of the Intelligence Community. President Trump's appointments of Robert F. Kennedy, Jr., Dr. Jay Bhattacharya, and Dr. Marty Makary present an opportunity for reform, but the pharmaceutical industry maintains its outsized and pernicious influence on government. Their liability shields remain intact, as do the corrupt arrangements of shared profiteering for public and private employees.

It remains to be seen whether President Trump and Elon Musk will be able to defeat, or even impair, the racket of taxpayer-funded NGOs that facilitated the destruction of 2020. The US has continued its development of quarantine camps, and pandemic frauds remain unrecovered. In March 2025, the Supreme Court denied President Trump, the head of the Executive Branch, the ability to halt foreign aid payments in a 5-4 decision, demonstrating the Chief Justice's continued subservience to the D.C. establishment.

Many people have learned, lost faith in authority, and swear that they will not comply next time. It's not so easy for industries who must comply or else lose their right to do business. When the health inspector tells the chicken farmer to slaughter his stock because of a PCR test, not complying will only lead to permanent closure. In other words, the lockdowns and mandates can easily come not through the front door but through the backdoor, basement, or attic.

It is an undeniable truth that the entire machine that unleashed mayhem is still in place. The industrial interests that pushed all these schemes still retain their access. The laws in states and the federal government have not been changed. Indeed, the quarantine camps could appear and be deployed in an instant with no real institutional blocks, and people can be rounded up and put there for reasons of politics masked as health concerns.

More optimistically, however, the resistance to lockdowns, mandates, and madness brought millions together in a coalition against tyranny. It raised awareness to the pestilent forces in our society that so many assumed were latent. The threat to fundamental rights led that amalgamation of political forces to reconsider and reaffirm the value of the first principles it had largely taken for granted. A jolt has awoken the somnambulant saunter of post-War America, creating the potential for real reform.

For now, however, that's all there is: potential. And there is no clear indication as to the direction of that future. The President who oversaw lockdowns and Operation Warp Speed built a coalition of dissidents in his return to the White House. His second cabinet appears remarkably more resilient than the advisors of his first term. Alex Azar, Mike Pence, and Jared Kushner have departed the West Wing to make room for those who appear unphased by the uphill nature of the fight for liberty. The presence of RFK,

Jr., Elon Musk, Tulsi Gabbard, Jay Bhattacharya, and J.D. Vance represents a deliberate and monumental shift in the Executive Branch, but their capacity to make a lasting dent is still in doubt.

The perpetrators of all the outrages of the last five years, carefully documented in this series, have every hope of creating in the opposition the feel of victory without the reality. So far, the wins are pyrrhic and await instantion in budgets, laws, and practice.

These days remind one of the experience in Kabul, Afghanistan, following the US invasion in 2002. When the troops landed, the Taliban was nowhere to be seen; all the fighters headed to the hills to prepare for the long fight. George W. Bush declared victory. US troops eventually fled in panic, and the Taliban runs Afghanistan today.

ABOUT BROWNSTONE INSTITUTE

Brownstone Institute, established May 2021, is a publisher and research institute that places the highest value on the voluntary interaction of individuals and groups while minimizing the use of violence and force, including that which is exercised by public authority.

INDEX

INDEX

Published by Brownstone Institute
Austin, Texas

www.ingramcontent.com/pod-product-compliance
Lightning Source LLC
Chambersburg PA
CBHW021924190326
41519CB00009B/906